Change Forces

To Wendy

My Change Force

Change Forces
Probing the Depths of Educational Reform

Michael Fullan

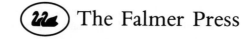 The Falmer Press

(A member of the Taylor & Francis Group)
London • New York • Philadelphia

UK   The Falmer Press, 4 John St., London WC1N 2ET
USA   The Falmer Press, Taylor & Francis Inc., 47 Runway Road, Suite G
Levittown, PA 19057

First Published 1993
Reprinted 1994, 1995, 1996, 1997, 1998, 2000

**A catalogue record for this book is available from the
British Library**

**Library of Congress Cataloguing in Publication Data are
available on request**

ISBN 1 85000 825 6 cased
ISBN 1 85000 826 4 paper

Jacket design by Gordon Pronk and Associates
Typeset in 11/13pt Bembo
by Graphicraft Typesetters Ltd., Hong Kong

Printed in Great Britain by Burgess Science Press, Basingstoke on
paper which has a specified pH value on final paper manufacture of
not less than 7.5 and is therefore 'acid free'.

Reprinted in the United States by Sheridan Books, Inc.

 Printed on recycled, acid free stock which meets the requirements of
the ANSI Standard Z39.48-1984 (Permanence of Paper).

Contents

Preface

'Change forces' is a deliberate double entendre. Change is ubiquitous and relentless, forcing itself on us at every turn. At the same time, the secret of growth and development is learning how to contend with the forces of change — turning positive forces to our advantage, while blunting negative ones. The future of the world is a learning future.

'Probing the depths of educational reform' is an apt sub-title. When you go deeper you go different. What appears to be a linear track becomes a new world. It is no longer sufficient to study factors associated with the success or failure of the latest innovation or policy. It is no longer acceptable to separate planned change from seemingly spontaneous or naturally occurring change. It is only by raising our consciousness and insights about the totality of educational change that we can do something about it. We will learn that it is not possible to solve 'the change problem', but we can learn to live with it more proactively and more productively. This is the theme of this book.

We are going to end up debunking myths, exposing half-truths, and juxtaposing things that do not normally go together. I will be calling into question vision and strategic planning, site-based management, strong leadership, accountability and assessment schemes, collegiality and consensus and other favorites of the day. It is no accident that these mis- and half-truths come equally from the left and the right because change of all kinds has certain generic properties in complex societies.

It is remarkable how far the study of educational change has come in the last thirty years, since it started in earnest in the 1960s. I will not review the evolution of this development (see Fullan, 1991) except to say that it has brought us to the beginning of a new phase which will represent a quantum leap — a paradigm breakthrough — in how we think about and act in relation to change. It is a world where change is a journey of unknown destination, where problems are our friends, where seeking assistance is a sign of strength, where simultaneous top-down bottom-up initiatives merge, where collegiality and individualism co-exist in productive tension (Fullan and Hargreaves, 1991; Fullan and Miles, 1992). It is a world where change mirrors *life itself* in which you can never be perfectly happy or permanently in harmony, but where some people (those with knowledge of how to view, cope with and initiate change) manage much better than others. It is a world where one should never trust a change agent, or never assume that others, especially leaders, know what they are doing — not because change agents and leaders are duplicitous or incompetent — but because the change process is so complex and so fraught with unknowns that all of us must be on guard and apply ourselves to investigating and solving problems.

It is a world where we will need generative concepts and capacities. What will be needed is the individual as inquirer and learner, mastery and know-how as prime strategies, the leader who expresses but also extends what is valued enabling others to do the same, team work and shared purpose which accepts both individualism and collectivism as essential to organizational learning, and the organization which is dynamically connected to its environment because that is necessary to avoid extinction as environments are always changing.

These are not brand-new concepts. The idea of the learning or self-renewing individual and organization has been around at least since the 1960s (Gardner, 1964). What is new is that we have much more depth of meaning; and despite the complexity of the ideas we have more of an intuitive and concrete grasp of how the concepts work in practice. We are beginning to appreciate more of the total picture. What appears simple is not so — introducing a seemingly small change turns out to have wild consequences. What appears complex is less so — enabling a few people to work on a difficult problem produces unanticipated windfalls. In the new science of chaos: 'Simple systems give rise to complex behaviour. Complex systems give rise to simple behaviour' (Gleick, 1987, p. 304). The trouble is that you cannot predict exactly when and how such consequences will happen. This is why we need more generative capacities that can anticipate and rise to the occasions of change on a continuous basis as they occur.

How do we know we are on the right track — this time? If we take the theme of this book seriously, we don't. There will be other accumulated tensions, insights and breakthroughs in the future. But there is considerable evidence to indicate that we are on the verge of one of those periodic breakthroughs. It is a time when new paradigm books appear, like *Managing on the Edge* (Pascale, 1990), *The Fifth Discipline* (Senge, 1990), *Flow* (Csikszentmihalyi, 1990), *Breakpoint and Beyond* (Land and Jarman, 1992), *The Critical Path to Corporate Renewal* (Beer, Eisenstat and Spector, 1990), *Managing the Unknowable* (Stacey, 1992), and *Voltaire's Bastards* (Saul, 1992). And it is a time when chronologically new, but paradigmatically old or wrong books, like *Changing the Essence* (Beckhard and Pritchard, 1992), *The Challenge of Organizational Change* (Kanter, Stein and Jick, 1992), and *Liberation Management* (Peters, 1992), stand out by comparison.

There comes a time in the cycles of societies where radical break-throughs or destruction are likely to occur. Change forces reach a breaking point. As we head toward the twenty-first century we are in such a period. Teachers' capacities to deal with change, learn from it, and help students learn from it will be critical for the future development of societies. They are not now in a position to play this vital role. We need a new mindset to go deeper. This book is an attempt to map out the basis for such a mindset to enable educators to become agents, rather than victims, of change.

The problems (and solutions) are worldwide (see Fullan, 1991; Dalin and Rolff, 1992; and Verspoor, 1989). I have been fortunate to have had change mentors and colleagues all over the world. There are too many to mention them all. I would like to thank several in particular, who have helped me learn. Matt Miles has been there every decade with his wisdom and insights. Co-authoring with him is a ticket to learning. Per Dalin opened up the international world of learning for me, and many others. Seymour Sarason introduced me to the phenomenon of change through his brilliant writings. Michael Huberman and Bruce Joyce are inspiring friends and colleagues, always raising fresh questions which result in new productive lines of inquiry. Milbrey McLaughlin and Judith Little continue to go deeper and deeper benefitting us all. Robert Baker, Ray Bolam, David Hopkins, Lawrence Ingvarson and Geoff Scott have been great international friends and change agents in their own right. David Crandall, Susan Loucks-Horsley and others at the Network persist as exemplars at integrating policy and practice. Michael Connelly, Nancy Watson and Ann Kilcher have been enormously productive colleagues and co-authors. Ken Leithwood has been a superb comrade in arms from the early days. Andy Hargreaves is a wonderful co-author, linking his analytical prowess with strategies for change. Bernard Shapiro taught me that the world of action is the real arena of change, and that you don't have to study change to know a lot about it. Bob Wiele has been a great source of ideas and advice. Thanks to Noel Clark and Linda Grant for giving me the concept and the challenge of 'What's Worth Fighting For'. Frank Clifford, Charles Pascal and Margaret Wilson have been great friends and supporters while tackling changes of enormous proportions in their own arenas of public policy.

Alliances and partnerships, as I take up in chapter 5, are major vehicles for learning. Our Learning Consortium is a powerful force for practitioners and academics to learn from each other while attempting to construct learning organizations together. Universities, school districts and schools work together to forge new environments for change. My sincere thanks to all the leaders in the Learning Consortium — and there are very many — for providing an exciting and productive living laboratory of change. I have also been privileged to be a member of the Directors' Study Group which is one of those all too rare opportunities for integrating personal and institutional learning in a challenging and supportive set of personal relationships.

My colleagues at the Faculty of Education, University of Toronto — engaged collectively in the very forces of change described in this book — represent to me the critical mass to go 'beyond the breakpoint' in reforming teacher education: from the forty-five faculty who have worked on the issue for the past twenty years, to the thirty new faculty who have joined them, to the 1100 academically and experientially rich student teachers each year, to our two lab schools, the Institute of Child Study, and the University of Toronto Schools, and to our President, Rob Prichard, a strong proponent of teacher education. We are now seeing a convergence of ideas and energy powerful enough to make a difference. Barrie Bennett and Carol Rolheiser-Bennett keep showing me how to blend theory and practice. Steve Anderson and Suzie Stiegelbauer are applied researchers *par excellence*. Many others at the Faculty are throwing themselves headlong and heartwide into redesigning teacher education. Mary Stager manages to be everything — executive assistant, advisor, problem-solver, researcher and co-author. Anne Millar and Dennis Thiessen have been tremendous personal supporters and leaders at the Faculty. The dynamic duo, Claudia Cuttress and Wendy Chiswell, managed a tremendous volume of work, while putting this manuscript to bed with great dispatch.

Balancing work and life, as I shall take up later in the book, is always a problem. This book has given me greater insight into the conclusion that being better at life and better at work go hand in hand. You can't have one without the other for very long. Chris, Maureen, Josh, Bailey and Conor — may the forces of change be with you. For Wendy, the dedication of this book says it all.

Chapter 1

The Problem and the Potential of Educational Change

The faithful witness . . . is at his[her] best when he[she] concentrates on questioning and avoids the specialist's obsession with solutions.
Saul, *Voltaire's Bastards* 1992

We have been fighting an uphill battle. For the past thirty years we have been trying to up the ante in getting the latest innovations and policies into place. We started naively in the 1960s pouring scads of money into large-scale national curriculum efforts, open plan schools, individualized instruction; and the like. It was assumed, but not planned for, that something was bound to come of it. We have never really recovered from the profound disappointment experienced when our expectations turned out to be so far removed from the realities of implementation. Indeed, the term implementation was not even used in the 1960s, not even contemplated as a problem.

That world of innocent expectations came crashing down around 1970 when the first implementation studies surfaced. People, especially those in the trenches, no doubt already knew something was terribly wrong, but the problem crystallized almost overnight in Goodlad *et al's* (1970), Gross *et al's* (1971) and Sarason's (1971) major studies of failed implementation.

There followed a period of stagnation, recovery and regrouping during most of the 1970s. Educators, especially in the first part of the decade, had a crisis of confidence. Perhaps the educational system and its inhabitants are not open to or capable of change? Perhaps, worse still, education, even if it improved, could not make a difference given social class, family and other societal conditions outside the purview of the educational sector?

As people plugged away, a few glimmers of hope came through. By the end of the 1970s the effective schools movement had accumulated some evidence, and a growing ideology that schools can make a difference even under trying conditions. The studies of implementation success and school improvement corroborated the spirit if not all the details of these findings. On another front, intensive work on inservice and staff development by Bruce Joyce and others demonstrated that ongoing competence-building strategies can work. By 1980 we could say that we knew a fair amount about the major factors associated with introducing single innovations.

From a societal point of view this was too little, too late. As problems in society worsened, the educational system was tinkering. Even its so-called successes were isolated — the exception rather than the rule. And they were not convincingly related to greater student learning. There was no confidence that we should, let alone could, reproduce these minor successes on a wider scale.

By the early 1980s, society had had enough. By about 1983 — in fact, the date is precise in the United States with the release of *A Nation at Risk* — the solution was seen as requiring large-scale governmental action. Structural solutions through top-down regulations were introduced in many of the Western countries. In many of the states in the US — intensively so in some states — curricula were specified and mandated, competencies for students and teachers were detailed and tested, salaries of teachers (woefully low at the time) were raised, leadership competencies were listed and trained. Other countries (although Canada is much more uneven given provincial autonomy) paralleled these developments. In Great Britain for example, the Education Reform Act of 1988, heretically for that country, introduced a National Curriculum. Now we were engaged in large-scale tinkering.

Overlapping these top-down regulatory efforts was another movement which began after 1985. In the US it goes under the name of restructuring (Elmore, 1990; Murphy, 1991). Here the emphasis is on school-based management, enhanced roles for principals and teachers, and other decentralized components.

The present is a combination of bifurcation and confusion. The former is represented on the one hand, by centralists who see greater top-down regulation, accountability and control of the educational establishment as the answer. This includes, by the way, strategies such as local management of schools which attempt to place more power in the hands of local interests outside the school. The other hand of bifurcation is represented by the restructionists who see greater control by school-based teachers and other educators as the basic solution.

Many of the bifurcators are deeply convinced that they are right. Unfortunately they offer opposite solutions. For most of us, confusion seems to be the most warranted state of mind in the early 1990s. The ante has been upped in that we are no longer considering particular innovations one at a time, but rather more comprehensive reforms. It has also been upped in that the solution is seen as too important to leave to educators. Governments (not just Ministries of Education) and business interests are now major players.

We are, in other words, engaged in higher stakes solutions with more to win, but also more to lose. It does not seem to be a good time to wallow in confusion. Tinkering after all can be on a small or large scale, its main characteristic being 'a clumsy attempt to mend something' (*Webster's New World Dictionary*).

I maintain that we have been fighting an ultimately fruitless uphill battle. The solution is not how to climb the hill of getting more innovations or reforms into the educational system. We need a different formulation to get at the heart of the problem, a different hill, so to speak. We need, in short, a new mindset about educational change.

A New Mindset for Change

Senge (1990) reminds us that the Greek word *metanoia* means 'a fundamental shift of mind'. This is what we need about the concept of educational change itself. Without such a shift of mind the insurmountable basic problem is the juxtaposition of a continuous *change theme* with a continuous *conservative system*. On the one hand, we have the constant and ever expanding presence of educational innovation and reform. It is no exaggeration to say that dealing with change is endemic to post-modern society. On the other hand, however, we have an educational system which is fundamentally conservative. The way that teachers are trained, the way that schools are organized, the way that the educational hierarchy operates, and the way that education is treated by political decision-makers results in a system that is more likely to retain the *status quo* than to change. When change is attempted under such circumstances it results in defensiveness, superficiality or at best short-lived pockets of success.

To put it differently, the answer does not lie in designing better reform strategies. No amount of sophistication in strategizing for particular innovations or policies will ever work. It is simply unrealistic to expect that introducing reforms one by one, even major ones, in a situation which is basically not organized to engage in change will do anything but give reform a bad name. You cannot have an educational environment in which change is continuously expected, alongside a conservative system and expect anything but constant aggravation.

The new problem of change, then, pursued in this book is what would it take to make the educational system a learning organization — expert at dealing with change as a normal part of its work, not just in relation to the latest policy, but as a way of life. In subsequent chapters we will examine the constituent components necessary for this change. The reason that we need learning organizations is related to the discovery that change in complex systems is nonlinear — full of surprises. Yet new mindsets can help us 'manage the unknowable' (Stacey, 1992).

We must also ask at the outset why is it important that education develop such a change capacity, or if you like, what is the promise of educational change if it were to get that good. One could respond at the abstract level that change is all around us, the self-renewing society is essential, education must produce critical thinkers and problem solvers etc. but these have become cliches. A deeper reason, which is the subject of chapter 2, is that education has a moral purpose. The moral purpose is to make a difference in the lives of students regardless of background, and to help produce citizens who can live and work productively in increasingly dynamically complex societies. This is not new either, but what is new, I think, is the realization that to do this puts teachers precisely in the business of continuous innovation and change. They are, in other words, in the business of *making improvements*, and to make improvements in an ever changing world is to contend with and manage the forces of change on an ongoing basis.

Productive educational change is full of paradoxes, and components that are often not seen as going together. Caring and competence, equity and excellence, social and economic development are not mutually exclusive. On the contrary, these tensions must be reconciled into powerful new forces for growth and development.

The full outline of the argument goes something like this. Society — for some time now, but increasingly moreso as we head to the twenty-first century — expects its citizens to be capable of proactively dealing with change throughout life both individually as well as collaboratively in a context of dynamic, multicultural global transformation. Of all the institutions in society, education is the only one that *potentially* has the promise of fundamentally contributing to this goal. Yet, education far from being a hotbed of teaching people to deal with change in basic ways is just the opposite. To break through this impasse, educators must see themselves and be seen as experts in the dynamics of change. To become expert in the dynamics of change, educators — administrators and teachers alike — must become skilled change agents. If they do become skilled change agents with moral purpose, educators will make a difference in the lives of students from all backgrounds, and by so doing help produce greater capacity in society to cope with change.

This is not one of these goals that you can tinker with, that you can vaguely or obliquely expect to happen or that you can accomplish by playing it safe. The goal of greater change capacity must become explicit and its pursuit must become all out and sustained.

One could argue that we don't have much choice. At one level this is true. Few would deny that the ability to deal with change is one of the premier requisites of the present and future. But neither individuals nor groups are known for doing what is best for them, especially when the stakes are high. The historian Barbara Tuchman (1984) exposes this tendency in a grand historical sweep in the *The March of Folly*. Taking as cases in point, the Trojans, the Renaissance Popes, the British loss of America, and the American loss in Vietnam, Tuchman examines her basic thesis 'The Pursuit of Policy Contrary to Self-Interest'. For Tuchman a policy to qualify as folly had to meet three criteria: 'it must have been perceived (by some) as counter-productive in its own time . . . a feasible alternative course of action must have been available . . . the policy in question should be that of a group, not an individual ruler' (p. 5). Among other factors Tuchman cites 'Obliviousness to the growing disaffection of constituents, primacy of self-aggrandizement, illusion of invulnerable status' as persistent aspects of folly (p. 126) (see also CRM Films, *Groupthink*, 1992). Thus, those in authority are unlikely by themselves to conceive of alternative courses of action, even (perhaps especially) when faced with overwhelming problems.

Moral purpose is one antidote to the march of folly, but it is martyrdom without the inbuilt capacity — the habits and skills required — to engage in continuous corrective analysis and action. Productive educational change at its core, is not the capacity to implement the latest policy, but rather the ability to survive the vicissitudes of planned and unplanned change while growing and developing.

Educators cannot do the task alone. Already too much is expected of them. Teachers' jobs are more complex than ever before. They must respond to the needs of a diverse and changing student population, a rapidly changing technology in the workplace, and demands for excellence from all segments of society. The global marketplace raises the stakes ever higher in its performance demands of schools. Deteriorating social conditions continue to widen the awful gap between the haves and have nots. As Goodlad (1992a) says, 'healthy nations have healthy schools' not the other way around. Many things are required for a nation to be healthy, observes Goodlad:

Education in parenting, an array of agencies and institutions including schools joined in an educative ecology, a business/ corporate ethos of making the highest quality goods available at the lowest possible cost, a substantial investment in research and development, leaders and executive officers who rise to the top through first-rate performance in all aspects of the enterprise, and more. (pp. 7–8; see also, Goodlad, 1992b)

We are talking about the larger social agenda of creating learning societies. The focus of change must be on all agencies and their inter-relationships, but education has a special obligation to help lead the way in partnership with others.

Overview of the Book

In chapter 2 I take up the rather strange partnership of moral purpose and change agentry. On closer inspection they are natural companions in the post-modern age. Moral purpose without change agentry is so much wishful valuing; change agentry without moral purpose is change for the sake of change. It is not farfetched to conceive of teachers as change agents. They are already part way there. Teachers as change agents is the *sine qua non* of getting anywhere.

Chapter 3 delves into the complexity of the change process, identifying insights not previously possible with the old mindset of policy and program implementation. Lessons for understanding change in new ways will be identified in order to provide more generative concepts for contending with the forces of change. We will see how seemingly incompatible pairs like continuity and change, personal mastery and collective action, vision and openness, failure and success, and pressure and support, not only can but also must go together in successful change processes.

Chapters 4 and 5 focus respectively on the school as a learning organization, and on the two-way relationship between a learning organization and its environment. I do not assume that the school of the future will look like the school of today (or even be called a school). But using recent research and the generative concept of the learning organization, we can begin to see how the education organization of the future would function. How individualism and collaboration must co-exist. How vision and strategic planning have serious blind spots. How educators must work in new ways. In chapter 5 the relationship to the environment is explored again with new and I think fruitful results. Why neither centralization nor decentralization works. Why the best collaborative organizations are (and must be to survive) more open to and proactive with their environments. What external agencies must do to help produce and sustain learning organizations.

Teacher education defined as the entire continuum — the subject of chapter 6 — has the honour of being the best solution and the worst problem in education today. Despite the rhetoric, society has not yet seriously tried to use teacher education as a tool for improvement. Underneath the rhetoric there does not seem to be a real belief or confidence that investing in teacher education will yield results. Building on the analysis of previous chapters, I will argue that the problem of productive change simply cannot be addressed unless we treat continuous teacher education — pre-service and in-service — as the major vehicle for producing teachers as moral change agents.

In the final chapter, I return to the individual and change in societal context. Especially in times of paradigm or mindset shifts we cannot expect existing institutions to lead the way. More fundamentally, in any society of the future, productive educational change will mean productive individuals who do not fully trust the institutions that surround them. Systems do not change themselves, people change them. The role of the individual, the kind of institutions he or she should be helping to shape and check, and strategies for taking action along these lines will form the content of chapter 7.

To return to Tuchman, there are feasible alternative courses of action available. But we can't start from scratch each time there is a serious problem. We must ingrain in society the kind of capacity for educational change that inevitably generates its own checks and balances and lines of solution in situations that will always be somewhat out of control, even if we do everything right.

Chapter 2

Moral Purpose and Change Agentry

Managing moral purpose and change agentry is at the heart of productive educational change. It is necessary to take a closer look at each of them, and to make explicit their organic relationship.

Moral Purpose

In their major study of teacher education, Goodlad and his colleagues found themselves being pushed deeper to the moral purposes of education in order to understand the basic rationale for teaching in post-modern society: 'We came to see with increasing clarity the degree to which teaching in schools, public or private, carries with it *moral imperatives* — more in public schools, however, because they are not schools of choice in a system requiring compulsory schooling' (Goodlad, 1990a, p. 47, my emphasis; see also Goodlad, Soder and Sirotnik, 1990). Goodlad singles out four moral imperatives:

Facilitating Critical Enculturation

The school is the only institution in our nation specifically charged with enculturating the young into a political democracy . . . Schools are major players in developing educated persons who acquire an understanding of truth, beauty, and justice against which to judge their own and society's virtues and imperfections . . . This is a moral responsibility. (pp. 48–9)

Providing Access to Knowledge

The school is the only institution in our society specifically charged with providing to the young a disciplined encounter with all the subject matters of the human conversation: the world as a physical and biological system; evaluative and belief systems; communication systems; the social, political, and economic systems that make up the global village; and the human species itself . . . (Teachers) must be diligent in ensuring that no attitudes, beliefs, or practices bar students from access to the necessary knowledge. (p. 49)

Building an Effective Teacher-Student Connection

The moral responsibility of educators takes on its most obvious significance where the lives of teachers and their students intersect . . . The epistemology of teaching must encompass a pedagogy that goes far beyond the *mechanics* of teaching. It must combine generalizable principles of teaching, subject-specific instruction, sensitivity to the pervasive human qualities and potentials always involved. (pp. 49–50)

Practicing Good Stewardship

If schools are to become the responsive, renewing institutions that they must, the teachers in them must be purposefully engaged in the renewal process. (Goodlad, 1990b, p. 25)

One of Goodlad's colleagues, Sirotnik (1990, p. 298 ff) adds his list of moral requirements: commitment to *inquiry, knowledge, competence, caring, freedom, well-being, and social justice*. In his own words:

The implications of moral commitments to inquiry, knowledge, competence, caring, and social justice go farther than curriculum and classroom experiences. They go to the very heart of the moral ecology of the organization itself. This can be readily seen in the extent to which these commitments are reflected in the work environment of educators outside of classroom teaching *per se*. To what extent does the organizational culture encourage and support educators as inquirers into what they do and how they might do it better? To what extent do educators consume, critique, and produce knowledge? To what extent do they engage competently in discourse and action to improve the conditions, activities and outcomes, of schooling? To what extent do educators care about themselves and each other in the same way they care (or ought to care) about students? To what extent are educators empowered to participate authentically in pedagogical matters of fundamental importance — what schools are for and how teaching and learning can be aligned with this vision. (p. 312)

At a policy level, growing concerns about educational equity and economic performance mirror the more particular issues just described. The restructuring movement, in intent at least, places a renewed focus on the education of *all* students, 'especially those who have been in-effectively served in the past' and attempts to reorganize schools for that purpose (Murphy, 1991, p. 60). Poverty, especially among children and women, racism, drug abuse, and horrendous social and personal problems all make the equity and excellence agenda more serious and poignant day by day (Hodgkinson, 1991).

My main point, however, is not to consider these matters at the institutional level — at least not at this time. The building block is the moral purpose of the *individual* teacher. Scratch a good teacher and you will find a moral purpose. At the Faculty of Education, University of Toronto, we recently examined why student teachers wanted to enter the profession. We have a post-baccalaureate fifth year program which results in certification after one year. It represents a particularly select group because there is a great demand to enter teaching in Ontario. For 1992/93 there were some 7000 applicants for 1100 positions. We use as admission criteria a combination of two factors weighted equally — academic grades, and an applicant 'profile' designed to capture experience and reasons for entering teaching. Because of the emphasis on experience, the average age is 29. In a small study we drew a random sample of 20 per cent of those in the 1991/92 year (Stiegelbauer, 1992). We set out to derive from the written profiles, what student teachers said about 'why they want to become teachers'. The most frequently mentioned theme was 'I want to make a difference' reflected in the following sample of quotes:

I hope my contribution to teaching, along with other good teachers' contributions, will help result in a better society for our future. I care about children and the way that children are learning.

Education is an important factor which determines the quality of an individual life and the future of society as a whole.

No other profession enables one the opportunity to provide such a positive impact on a child's overall development.

I want to effect positive change in students' lives.

I've always thought that if I could go into a classroom and make a difference in one kid's life . . . then that's what I am here for.

I am not suggesting that the mere statement of purpose is a straightforward matter. We cannot automatically take these statements at face value (although our day-to-day experience with student teachers provides ample corroboration of this theme), and there are different motivations for entering teaching among any cohort: But I am saying that we have a kernel of truth here. Many, many teachers enter the profession because they want to make a contribution — they want to make a difference!

What happens here-on-in — in teacher preparation, induction, and throughout the career — is a different story. Those with a non-existent or limited sense of moral purpose are never called upon to demonstrate their commitment. Those with moral potential, however inchoate, are never developed. Those with a clearer sense of purpose are thwarted.

Hargreaves and Tucker (1991) address the latter issues in their treatment of teaching and guilt. They quote Davies (1989, p. 49) 'at the centre of the feeling of guilt is self disappointment, a sense of having done badly, fallen short, of having betrayed a personal ideal, standard or commitment'. Hargreaves and Tucker (1991) also suggest that aspects of moral purpose like caring may be too narrowly conceived. They argue that there is more to it than personal caring and interpersonal sharing: 'Care . . . carries with it social and moral responsibilities as well as interpersonal ones' (p. 12).

The argument is somewhat subtle, so let me make it more directly. If concerns for making a difference remain at the one-to-one and classroom level, it cannot be done. An additional component is required. Making a difference, must be explicitly recast in broader social and moral terms. It must be seen that one cannot make a difference at the interpersonal level unless the problem and solution are enlarged to encompass the conditions that surround teaching (such as the collaborative school, chapter 4), and the skills and actions that would be needed to make a difference. Without this additional and broader dimension the best of teachers will end up as moral martyrs. In brief, care must be linked to a broader social, public purpose, and the latter if it is to go anywhere must be propelled by the skills of change agentry.

We now come to the integrative theme of the chapter: *teachers are agents of educational change and societal improvement*. This is not as highfalutin as it sounds. I have already argued that they are part way there on a small scale with their aspirations for making a difference. And they are there ecologically with expectations of reform constantly swirling around them. In addition to making moral purpose more explicit (thereby clearly declaring what business we are in) educators also need the tools to engage in change productively. Care and competence, equity and excellence, social and economic development are natural allies in this quest.

Change Agentry

I will have more to say about change agentry later. Here I want to outline some of its elements at the individual level. How to produce more of it, and under what conditions it can be further developed and sustained are the subjects of the remaining chapters.

I define change agentry as being self-conscious about the nature of change and the change process. Those skilled in change are appreciative of its semi-unpredictable and volatile character, and they are explicitly concerned with the pursuit of ideas and competencies for coping with and influencing more and more aspects of the process toward some desired set of ends. They are open, moreover, to discovering new ends as the journey unfolds. In chapter 3, the complexities of the change process and some of the insights and lessons arising from the new mindset will be explored in detail. At this stage the question is, what conceptions and skills should the teacher of moral purpose possess in order to become a more effective change agent.

I see four core capacities required as a generative foundation for building greater change capacity: personal vision-building, inquiry, mastery, and collaboration. Each of these has its institutional counterpart: shared vision-building, organizational structures, norms and practices of inquiry; focus on organizational development and know-how, and collaborative work cultures (chapter 4). For reasons that should be increasingly clear throughout this book we need a dual approach working simultaneously on individual and institutional development. One cannot wait for the other. And if they are not working in concert, in particular settings, it is necessary to work on them separately looking for opportunities to make them connect.

The individual educator is a critical starting point because the leverage for change can be greater through the efforts of individuals, and each educator has some control (more than is exercised) over what he or she does, because it is one's own motives and skills that are at question. Moreover, working individually on the four capacities about to be described makes it inevitable that there will be plenty of intersection of effort. I am not talking about leaders as change agents (more of that later) but of a more basic message: *each and every educator must strive to be an effective change agent.*

I start with personal vision-building because it connects so well with moral purpose contending with the forces of change. Shared vision is important in the long run, but for it to be effective you have to have something to share. It is not a good idea to borrow someone else's vision. Working on vision means examining and reexamining, and making explicit to ourselves why we came into teaching. Asking 'What difference am I trying to make personally'? Is a good place to start. For most of us it will not be trying to create something out of nothing. The reasons are there, but possibly buried under other demands or through years of disuse, or for the beginning teacher still underdeveloped. It is time to make them front and centre. We should not think of vision as something only for leaders. It is not a farfetched concept. It arises by pushing ourselves to articulate what is important to us as educators. Block (1987) emphasizes that 'creating a vision forces us to take a stand for a preferred future' (p. 102); it signifies our disappointment with what exists now. To articulate our vision of the future 'is to come out of the closet with our doubts about the organization and the way it operates' (p. 105). Indeed, it forces us to come out of the closet with doubts about ourselves and what we are doing.

Says Block writing more generally about organizations: 'We all have strong values about doing work that has meaning, being of real service to our customers, treating other people well, and maintaining some integrity in the way we work' (p. 123). Teachers, as I have indicated, are in one of the most 'natural' occupations for working on purpose and vision, because underneath that is what teaching is all about.

Several points in conclusion. First, I cannot stress enough that personal purpose and vision are the starting agenda. It comes from within, it gives meaning to work, and it exists independent of the particular organization or group we happen to be in.

Second, personal vision in teaching is too often implicit and dormant. It is often expressed negatively (what people want to get rid of, or not see happen) or narrowly in terms of means (more time, smaller classes). We need also to have positive images as driving forces. Teachers do not have to wallow in hubris in realizing that they are in a strategic position. Teachers should be pursuing moral purpose with greater and greater skill, conceptualizing their roles on a higher plane than they currently do.

Third, once it gets going, personal purpose is not as private as it sounds. Especially in moral occupations like teaching, the more one takes the risk to express personal purpose, the more kindred spirits one will find. A great deal of overlap will be experienced. Good ideas converge under conditions of communication, and collaboration. Individuals will find that they can convert their own desires into social agendas with others. Remember, personal purpose is not just self-centered, it has social dimensions as well such as working effectively with others, developing better citizens, and the like.

Fourth, personal purpose in teaching should be pushed and pushed until it makes a connection to social betterment in society. This is what it is at the one-to-one teacher-student level anyway. It has greater scope and meaning, and calls for wider action if we realize that *societal improvement* is really what education is about.

Fifth, and an extension of the previous point, is the realization that personal purpose in teaching is a *change theme*. Gardner (1964, p. 72) quotes Petrarch

> By citizens, of course, I mean those who love the existing order; for those who daily desire change are rebels and traitors, and against such a stern justice may take its course.

Today, the teacher who works for or allows the *status quo* is the traitor. Purposeful change is the new norm in teaching. It has been bouncing around within teaching for the past thirty years. It is time we realized that teachers above all are moral change agents in society — a role that must be pursued explicitly and aggressively.

Finally, and paradoxically, personal purpose is the route to *organizational* change. When personal purpose is diminished we see in its place groupthink and a continual stream of fragmented surface, ephemeral innovations. We see in a phrase, the uncritical acceptance of innovation, the more things change, the more they remain the same. When personal purpose is present in numbers it provides the power for deeper change:

> Cultures get changed in a thousand small ways, not by dramatic announcements from the boardroom. If we wait until top management gives leadership to the change we want to see, we miss the point. For us to have any hope that our own preferred future will come to pass, we provide the leadership. (Block, 1987, pp. 97–8).

All four capacities of change agentry are intimately interrelated and mutually reinforcing. The second one — inquiry — is to say that the formation and enactment of personal purpose is not a static matter. It is a perennial quest. One of the new paradigm writers, Richard Pascale (1990) captures this precisely: '*The* essential activity for keeping our paradigm current is persistent questioning. I will use the term *inquiry*. Inquiry is the engine of vitality and self-renewal' (p. 14). Stacey (1992) puts it this way: 'A successful, innovative organization must have groups of people who can perform complex learning spontaneously. Because in open-ended situations no one can know what the group is trying to learn, the learning process must start without a clear statement of what is to be learned or how' (p. 112).

Inquiry is necessary at the outset for forming personal purpose. While the latter comes from within, it must be fueled by information, ideas, dilemmas and other contentions in our environment. The beginner, by definition, is not experienced enough with the variety and needs of students, and with the operational goals and dilemmas of improvement to have clear ideas of purpose. Habits of 'questioning, experimentation, and variety' are essential (*ibid*). Reflective practice, personal journals, action research, working in innovative mentoring and peer settings are some of the strategies currently available (see Fullan and Hargreaves, 1991). Inquiry means internalizing norms, habits and techniques for *continuous learning*.

Learning is critical for the beginning teacher because of its formative timing. But we are talking about more than this — lifelong inquiry is the generative characteristic needed because post-modern environments themselves are constantly changing. We are probably never exactly right in the first place, but in any case we need the checks and balances of inquiry because in changing times our initial mental maps 'cease to fit the territory' (Pascale, 1990, p. 13). Thus, we need mechanisms to question and update our mental maps on a continuous basis. For Pascale, the question is the answer: 'Our quest isn't just a New Management Paradigm of the Nineties but a way of thinking that is continually open to the next paradigm and the next and the next . . .' (p. 265). What could be closer to change agentry?

The relationship between the first two capacities — personal vision and inquiry — involves the ability to simultaneously *express and extend* what you value. The genesis of change arises from this dynamic tension.

The capacity of mastery is another crucial ingredient. People must behave their way into new ideas and skills, not just think their way into them. Mastery and competence are obviously necessary for effectiveness, but they are also *means* (not just outcomes) for achieving deeper understanding. New mindsets arise from new mastery as much as the other way around. Mastery then is very much interrelated with vision and inquiry as is evident in this passage from Senge (1990):

> Personal mastery goes beyond competence and skills, though it is grounded in competence and skills . . . It means approaching one's life as a creative work, living life from a creative as opposed to a reactive viewpoint . . .
>
> When personal mastery becomes a discipline — an activity we integrate into our lives — it embodies two underlying movements. The first is continually clarifying what is important to us (purpose and vision). We often spend too much time coping with problems along our path that we forget why we are on that path in the first place. The result is that we only have a dim, or even inaccurate, view of what's really important to us.
>
> The second is continually learning how to see current reality more clearly . . . The juxtaposition of vision (what we want) and a clear picture of current reality (where we are relative to what we want) generates what we call 'creative tension'. 'Learning' in this context does not mean acquiring more information, but expanding the ability to produce results we truly want in life. It is lifelong generative learning. (p. 142)

It has long been known that skill and know-how are central to successful change, so it is surprising how little attention we pay to it beyond one-shot workshops and disconnected training. Mastery involves strong initial teacher education, and continuous staff development throughout the career, but it is more than this when we place it in the perspective of comprehensive change agentry. It is a learning habit that permeates everything we do. It is not enough to be exposed to new ideas. We have to know where new ideas fit, and we have to become skilled in them, not just like them.

Block (1987) says that the goal is:

> (to learn) as much as you can about the activity you are engaged in. There's pride and satisfaction in understanding your function better than anyone else and better than you thought possible. (p. 86)

We also know that inquiry, learning, and mastery are intrinsically anxiety producing: 'Almost every important learning experience we have ever had has been stressful. Those issues that create stress for us give us clues about the uncooked seeds within us that need attention' (*ibid*, p. 191). This means that the capacity to suspend belief, take risks, and experience the unknown are essential to learning. We can be more selective in what we try (as distinct from accepting all change) but in exploring selected new ideas we must be patient enough to learn more about them and to look for longer term consequences before drawing conclusions.

Rosenholtz (1989) found that teachers in schools characterized by these 'learning enriched' habits, not only learned more and became better at what they did, but they became more confident. The more accustomed one becomes at dealing with the unknown, the more one understands that creative breakthroughs are always preceded by periods of cloudy thinking, confusion, exploration, trial and stress; followed by periods of excitement, and growing confidence as one pursues purposeful change, or copes with unwanted change.

Back to Senge (1990):

People with a high level of personal mastery live in a continual learning mode . . . personal mastery is not something you possess. It is a process. It is a lifelong discipline. People with a high level of personal mastery are acutely aware of their ignorance, their incompetence, their growth areas. And they are deeply self-confident. Paradoxical? Only for those who do not see that 'the journey is the reward'. (p. 142)

In order to be effective at change, mastery is essential, both in relation to specific innovations and as a personal habit. New competencies and know-how are requirements for better understanding and judging the new and are the route to greater effectiveness.

Collaboration is the fourth capacity. Aside from the power of collaboration which we take up in later chapters collaboration is essential for personal learning (Fullan and Hargreaves, 1991). There is a ceiling effect to how much we can learn if we keep to ourselves. The ability to collaborate — on both a small and large scale — is becoming one of the core requisites of postmodern society. Personal strength, as long as it is open minded (i.e., inquiry oriented) goes hand-in-hand with effective collaboration — in fact, without personal strength collaboration will be more form than content. Personal mastery and group mastery feed on each other in learning organizations. People need one another to learn and to accomplish things.

Small-scale collaboration involves the attitude and capacity to form productive mentoring and peer relationships, team building and the like. On a larger scale, it consists of the ability to work in organizations that form cross-institutional partnerships such as school district, university and school-community and business agency alliances, as well as global relationships with individuals and organizations from other cultures.

In short, without collaborative skills and relationships it is not possible to learn and to continue to learn as much as you need in order to be an agent for societal improvement.

In summary, skills in change agentry are needed, because the processes of improvement are dynamically complex, and as we shall see, these processes are to a certain extent unknowable in advance. Chaos in a scientific sense is not disorder, but a process in which contradictions and complexities play themselves out coalescing into clusters (see Gleick, 1987, Stacey, 1992, Wheatley, 1992). Scientists talk about 'strange attractors' as forces that pull chaotic states into periodic patterns. Moral purpose is one of change processes' strange attractors because the pursuit and pull of meaning can help organize complex phenomena as they unfold. Strange attractors do not guide the process (because it is not guidable), they capitalize on it. Without moral purpose, aimlessness and fragmentation prevail. Without change agentry, moral purpose stagnates. The two are dynamically inter-related, not only because they need each other, but because they quite literally *define* (and redefine) each other as they interact.

I have argued that moral purpose and change agentry, far from being strange bedfellows, should be married. They keep each other honest. They feed on, and fulfill one another. Moreover, together they are generative in that they have an in-built capacity to self-correct and to continually refigure what should be done. Not only are they effective at getting things done, but they are good at getting the *right* things done.

I have also claimed that moral purpose and change agentry separately, but especially in combination, are as yet society's great untapped resources for improvement. We need to make them explicit, and make them part and parcel of personal and collective agendas. We need to go public with a new rationale for why teaching and teacher development is so fundamental to the future of society. We need to begin to practice on a wide scale what is implicit in the moral purpose of teaching. To do so we need the capacities of change agentry. And we need to know a lot more about the complexities of the change process.

Chapter 3

The Complexity of the Change Process

Productive educational change roams somewhere between overcontrol and chaos (Pascale, 1990). There are fundamental reasons why controlling strategies don't work. The underlying one is that the change process is uncontrollably complex, and in many circumstances 'unknowable' (Stacey, 1992). The solution lies in better ways of thinking about, and dealing with, inherently unpredictable processes.

How is change complex? Take any educational policy or problem and start listing all the forces that could figure in the solution and that would need to be influenced to make for productive change. Then, take the idea that unplanned factors are inevitable — government policy changes or gets constantly redefined, key leaders leave, important contact people are shifted to another role, new technology is invented, immigration increases, recession reduces available resources, a bitter conflict erupts, and so on. Finally, realize that every new variable that enters the equation — those unpredictable but inevitable noise factors — produce ten other ramifications, which in turn produces tens of other reactions and on and on.

As you think through the reality of the previous paragraph there is only one conclusion: 'No one could possibly come to figure out all these interactions' (Senge, 1990, p. 281). As one of Senge's participants exclaimed after being engaged in an exercise to map out all the complexities of a particular problem:

All my life, I assumed that somebody, somewhere knew the answer to this problem. I thought politicians knew what had to be done, but refused to do it out of politics and greed. But now I realize that nobody knows the answer. Not us, not them, not anybody. (p. 282)

Senge makes the distinction between 'detailed complexity' and 'dynamic complexity'. The former involves identifying all the variables that could influence a problem. Even this would be enormously difficult for one person or a group to orchestrate. But detailed complexity is not reality. Dynamic complexity is the real territory of change: 'when "cause and effect" are not close in time and space and obvious interventions do not produce expected outcomes' (*ibid*, p. 365) because other 'unplanned' factors dynamically interfere. And we keep discovering, as Dorothy in Oz did, that 'I have a feeling that we are not in Kansas anymore'. Complexity, dynamism, and unpredictability, in other words, are not merely things that get in the way. They are normal!

Stacey (1992) goes even further. Since change in dynamically complex circumstances is non-linear, we cannot predict or guide the process with any precision:

> While Senge concludes that cause and effect are distant from each other in complex systems and therefore difficult to trace, this chapter concludes that the linkage between cause and effect disappears and is therefore impossible to trace. (p. 78)

Stacey concludes:

> The long-term future of such organizations is completely unknowable because the links between specific actions and specific outcomes become lost in the detail of what happens. We can claim to have achieved something intentionally only when we can show that there was a connection between the specific action we took and the specific state we achieved; in other words, that what we achieved was not materially affected by chance. Since it is impossible to satisfy this condition when we operate in a chaotic system, it follows that successful human organizations cannot be the realization of some shared intention formed well ahead of action. Instead, success has to be the discovery of patterns that emerge through actions we take in response to the changing agendas of issues we identify. (p. 124)

What all this means is that productive change is the constant 'search for understanding, knowing there is no ultimate answer' (*ibid*, p. 282). The real leverage for change, says Senge involves:

- Seeing interrelationships rather than linear cause — effect chains, and
- Seeing processes of change rather than snapshots. (*ibid*, p. 73)

The goal then is to get into the habit of experiencing and thinking about educational change processes as an overlapping series of dynamically complex phenomena. As we develop a non-linear system language, new thinking about change emerges:

> The sub-conscious is subtly retrained to structure data in circles instead of lines. We find that we 'see' feedback processes and system archetypes everywhere. A new framework for thinking is embedded. A switch is thrown, much like what happens in mastering a foreign language. We begin to dream in the new language, or to think spontaneously in its terms and constraints. When this happens in systems thinking, we become . . . 'looped for life'. (*ibid*, p. 366)

Sounds complicated? Yes. Impractical? No. It is eminently more practical than our usual ways of introducing change, if for no other reason than that the latter does not work. Indeed, wrong solutions to complex problems nearly always make things worse (worse than if nothing had been done at all).

So, what is this new language for harnessing the forces of change? Chart 1 contains eight basic lessons arising from the new paradigm of dynamic change.[1] Each one is somewhat of a paradox and a surprise relative to our normal way of thinking about change. They go together as a set, as no one lesson by itself would be useful. Each lesson must benefit from the wisdom of the other seven.

CHART 1: The Eight Basic Lessons of the New Paradigm of Change

Lesson One: You Can't Mandate What Matters
(The more complex the change the less you can force it)
Lesson Two: Change is a Journey not a Blueprint
(Change is non-linear, loaded with uncertainty and excitement and sometimes perverse)
Lesson Three: Problems are Our Friends
(Problems are inevitable and you can't learn without them)
Lesson Four: Vision and Strategic Planning Come Later
(Premature visions and planning blind)
Lesson Five: Individualism and Collectivism Must Have Equal Power

	(There are no one-sided solutions to isolation and groupthink)
Lesson Six:	Neither Centralization Nor Decentralization Works (Both top-down and bottom-up strategies are necessary)
Lesson Seven:	Connection with the Wider Environment is Critical for Success (The best organizations learn externally as well as internally)
Lesson Eight:	Every Person is a Change Agent (Change is too important to leave to the experts, personal mind set and mastery is the ultimate protection)

Lesson 1: You Can't Mandate What Matters

(The more complex the change, the less you can force it.)

Mandates are important. Policymakers have an obligation to set policy, establish standards, and monitor performance. But to accomplish certain kinds of purposes — in this case, important educational goals — you cannot mandate what matters, because what really matters for complex goals of change are skills, creative thinking, and committed action (McLaughlin, 1990). Mandates are not sufficient and the more you try to specify them the more narrow the goals and means become. Teachers are not technicians.

To elaborate, you can effectively mandate things that (i) do not require thinking or skill in order to implement them; and (ii) can be monitored through close and constant surveillance. You can, for example, mandate the cessation of the use of the strap, or mandate a sales tax on liquor or petrol. These kinds of changes do not require skill on the part of implementers to comply; and provided that they are closely monitored they can be enforced effectively.

Even in the relatively simple case — detailed, not dynamic complexity — almost all educational changes of value require new (i) skills; (ii) behaviour; and (iii) beliefs or understanding (Fullan, 1991). Think of: computers across the curriculum, teachers' thinking and problem solving skills, developing citizenship and team work, integration of special education in regular classrooms, dealing with multiculturalism and racism, working with social agencies to provide integrated services, responding to all students in the classroom, cooperative learning, monitoring the performance of students. All of these changes, to be productive, require skills, capacity, commitment, motivation, beliefs and insights, and discretionary judgment on the spot. If there is one cardinal rule of change in human condition, it is that you cannot *make* people change. You cannot force them to think differently or compel them to develop new skills.

Marris (1975) states the problem this way:

> When those who have the power to manipulate changes act as if they have only to explain, and when their explanations are not at once accepted, shrug off opposition as ignorance or prejudice, they express a profound contempt for the meaning of lives other than their own. For the reformers have already assimilated these changes to their purposes, and worked out a reformulation which makes sense to them, perhaps through months or years of analysis and debate. If they deny others the chance to do the same, they treat them as puppets dangling by the threads of their own conceptions. (p. 166)

In addition to the introduction of more and more mandated requirements, there is the general expectation in education that more and more innovation is needed. School people often respond to this expectation in a knee-jerk fashion adopting the latest 'hot' items (site-based management, peer coaching and mentoring, restructuring, co-operative learning, whole language etc.) It is no denial of the potential worth of particular innovations to observe that unless deeper change in thinking and skills occur there will be limited impact. It is probably closer to the truth to say that the main problem in public education is not resistance to change, but the presence of too many innovations mandated or adopted uncritically and superficially on an *ad hoc* fragmented basis.

The result, as Pascale (1990) observes: 'not surprisingly, ideas acquired with ease are discarded with ease' (p. 20). New ideas of any worth to be effective require an in-depth understanding, and the development of skill and commitment to make them work. You cannot mandate these things. The only alternative that works is creating conditions that enable and press people to consider personal and shared visions, and skill development through practice over time. The more that mandates are used the more that fads prevail, the more that change is seen as superficial and marginal to the real purpose of teaching. The more that you 'tighten' mandates, the more that educational goals and means get narrowed, and consequently the less impact there is.

Lesson 1 says that the acid test of productive change is whether individuals and groups develop skills and deep understandings in relation to new solutions. It finds mandates wanting because they have no chance of accomplishing these substantial changes even for single policies let alone for the bigger goals of moral purpose and the reality of dynamic complexity. Mandates alter some things, but they don't affect what matters. When complex change is involved, people do not and cannot change by being told to do so. Effective change agents neither embrace nor ignore mandates. They use them as catalysts to reexamine what they are doing.

Lesson 2: Change is a Journey, Not a Blueprint

(Change is non-linear, loaded with uncertainty, and sometimes perverse.)

I have already made the case in this chapter that change is a never-ending proposition under conditions of dynamic complexity. Another reason that you can't mandate what matters, is that you don't know what is going to matter until you are into the journey. If change involved implementing single, well-developed, proven innovations one at a time, perhaps it could be blueprinted. But school districts and schools are in the business of implementing a bewildering array of multiple innovations and policies simultaneously. Moreover, restructuring reforms are so multifaceted and complex that solutions for particular settings cannot be known in advance. If one tries to match the complexity of the situation with complex implementation plans, the process becomes unwieldy, cumbersome and usually wrong.

I think of the school in England described by McMahon and Wallace (1992) engaged in school development planning. Experienced in the planning process, working together, and committed to the plan they produced, they nonetheless encountered a series of unanticipated problems: staff training sessions had to be postponed because of delays in the production of national guidelines; a training project had to be deferred because the teacher appointed to run it had left after six weeks, leaving a vacancy which could not be filled for several months; the headteacher became pregnant and arrangements had to made for a temporary replacement; the Government introduced a series of new changes that had to be accommodated — and on and on. I think of the group in the Maritimes in Canada with whom we were working who defined change as 'likened to a planned journey into uncharted waters in a leaky boat with a mutinous crew'.

Thus, a journey into the partially known or unknown is an apt metaphor. As we will see, so many of the other lessons feed into and corroborate this one. Even well developed innovations represent journeys for those encountering them for the first time. With skills and understanding at stake — never acquired easily — it could not be otherwise. Other more complex reforms represent even greater uncertainty because more is being attempted, but above all because the solution is not known in advance. 'Route and destination', says Stacey (1992), 'must be discovered though the journey itself if you wish to travel to new lands' (p. 1). In the face of unpredictable change, 'the key to success lies in the creative activity of making new maps'. (p. 1)

Under conditions of uncertainty, learning, anxiety, difficulties, and fear of the unknown are *intrinsic* to all change processes, especially at the early stages. One can see why a risk-taking mentality and climate are so critical. People will not venture into uncertainty unless they or others appreciate that difficulties are a natural part of any change scenario. And if people do not venture into uncertainty, no significant change will occur (see Lesson 3 — problems are our friends).

We know that early difficulties are guaranteed. The perverse part is that later stages are unpredictable as well. It is true that in cases of eventual success there are great highs, ecstatic feelings of accomplishment, and moments of deep personal satisfaction and well being. With greater moral purpose and change agent capacity (chapter 2) the chances are greater that there will be more successes than failures. But sometimes things get worse rather than better even if we are doing all the right things. And sometimes they get better, even if we are making mistakes. As dynamic complexity generates surprises, for better or for worse, there is an element of luck. Non-luck comes into play in how we relate to these unanticipated events, not in whether we can prevent them in the first place. Sometimes they will be overwhelmingly frustrating and bad, and we won't be able to do a thing about it. People who learn to control their inner experiences, while contending with the positive and negative forces of change will be able to determine the quality of their lives (Csikszentmihalyi, 1990). Productive educational change, like productive life itself, really is a journey that doesn't end until we do.

Lesson 3: Problems are our Friends

(Problems are inevitable, but the good news is that you can't learn or be successful without them.)

It follows from almost everything I have said that *inquiry* is crucial. Problems are endemic in any serious change effort; both within the effort itself and via unplanned intrusions. Problems are necessary for learning, but not without a capacity for inquiry to learn the right lessons.

It seems perverse to say that problems are our friends, but we cannot develop effective responses to complex situations unless we actively seek and confront the real problems which are in fact difficult to solve. Problems are our friends because it is only through immersing ourselves in problems that we can come up with creative solutions. Problems are the route to deeper change and deeper satisfaction. In this sense effective organizations 'embrace problems' rather than avoid them.

Too often change-related problems are ignored, denied, or treated as an occasion for blame and defense. Success in school change efforts is much more likely when problems are treated as natural, expected phenomena, and are looked for. Only by tracking problems can we understand what has to be done next in order to get what we want. Problems need to be taken seriously, not attributed to 'resistance' or the ignorance or wrong-headedness of others. Successful change management requires problem-finding techniques like 'worry lists', and regular review of problem-solving decisions at subsequent meetings to see what happened. Since circumstances and context are constantly changing, sometimes in surprising ways, an embedded spirit of constant inquiry is essential. Says Pascale (1990, p. 14) 'inquiry is the engine of vitality and self-renewal'.

Louis and Miles (1990) found that the least successful schools they studied engaged in 'shallow coping' — doing nothing, procrastinating, doing it the usual way, easing off, increasing pressure — while the successful schools went deeper to probe underlying reasons and to make more substantial interventions like comprehensive restaffing, continuous training, redesigning programs, and the like. Successful schools did not have fewer problems than other schools — they just coped with them better. Moreover, the absence of problems is usually a sign that not much is being attempted. Smoothness in the early stages of a change effort is a sure sign that superficial or trivial change is being substituted for substantial change attempts. Later on, once mastered, changes can produce incredible highs through seemingly easy effort. There is nothing like accomplished performance for increasing self-esteem and confidence to go to even greater heights.

Avoidance of real problems is the enemy of productive change because it is these problems that must be confronted for breakthroughs to occur. Senge (1990, p. 24) paints the negative case:

All too often, teams in business tend to spend their time fighting for turf, avoiding anything that will make them look bad personally, and pretending that everyone is behind the team's collective strategy — maintaining the *appearance* of a cohesive team. To keep up the image, they seek to squelch disagreement; people with serious reservations avoid stating them publicly, and joint decisions are watered-down compromises reflecting what everyone can live with, or else reflecting one person's view foisted on the group. If there is disagreement, it's usually expressed in a manner that lays blame, polarizes opinion, and fails to reveal the underlying differences in assumptions and experience in a way that the team as a whole could learn.

Problems are our friends is another way of saying that *conflict is essential* to any successful change effort:

People do not provoke new insights when their discussions are characterized by orderly equilibrium, conformity, and dependence. Neither do they do so when their discussions enter the explosively unstable equilibrium of all-out conflict or complete avoidance of issues . . . People spark new ideas off each other when they argue and disagree — when they are conflicting, confused, and searching for new meaning — yet remain willing to discuss and listen to each other. (Stacey, 1992, p. 120)

The proper way to deal with confusion, observes Saul (1992, p. 535), 'is to increase that confusion by asking uncomfortable questions until the source of the difficulties is exposed'. Yet we do the opposite by affirming rhetorical truths, and covering up conflict.

A pattern is beginning to emerge. Substantial change involves complex processes. The latter is inherently problem rich. A spirit of openness and inquiry is essential to solving problems. Change is learning. Pascale (1990, p. 263) summarizes why problems are our friends:

Life doesn't follow straight-line logic; it conforms to a kind of curved logic that changes the nature of things and often turns them into their opposites. Problems then, are not just hassles to be dealt with and set aside. Lurking inside each problem is a workshop on the nature of organizations and a vehicle for personal growth. This entails a shift; we need to value the *process* of finding the solution — juggling the inconsistencies that meaningful solutions entail.

In short, problems are our friends; but only if you do something about them.

Lesson 4: Vision and Strategic Planning Come Later

(Premature visions and planning can blind.)

Visions are necessary for success but few concepts are as misunderstood and misapplied in the change process. Visions come later for two reasons. First, under conditions of dynamic complexity one needs a good deal of reflective experience before one can form a plausible vision. Vision emerges from, more than it precedes, action. Even then it is always provisional. Second, *shared* vision, which is essential for success, must evolve through the dynamic interaction of organizational members and leaders. This takes time and will not succeed unless the vision-building process is somewhat open-ended. Visions coming later does not mean that they are not worked on. Just the opposite. They are pursued more authentically while avoiding premature formalization.

Visions come later because the process of merging personal and shared visions takes time. Senge (1990) provides an illuminating discussion of the tension between personal and collective ideals.

> Shared vision is vital for the learning organization because it provides the focus and energy for learning. While adaptive learning is possible without vision, generative learning occurs only when people are striving to accomplish something that matters deeply to them. In fact, the whole idea of generative learning — 'expanding your ability to create' — will seem abstract and meaningless *until* people become excited about some vision they truly want to accomplish.
>
> Today, 'vision' is a familiar concept in corporate leadership. But when you look carefully you find that most 'visions' are one person's (or one group's) vision imposed on an organization. Such visions, at best, command compliance — not commitment. A shared vision is a vision that many people are truly committed to, because it reflects their own personal vision. (p. 206)

And,

> Organizations intent on building shared visions continually
> encourage members to develop their personal visions. If people
> don't have their own vision, all they can do is 'sign up' for
> someone else's. The result is compliance, never commitment.
> On the other hand, people with a strong sense of personal
> direction can join together to create a powerful synergy toward
> what I/we truly want. (Senge, 1990, p. 211)

By contrast, the old and dead wrong paradigm is still being pro-
mulgated, such as Beckhard and Pritchard's (1992) recommendations
for vision-driven change. There are four key aspects, they say: creating
and setting the vision; communicating the vision; building commitment to the vision; and organizing people and what they do so that
they are aligned to the vision (p. 25). Not!

In their study of twenty-six plants over a five-year period, Beer,
Eisenstat and Spector (1990) conclude just the opposite:

> Change efforts that begin by creating corporate programs to
> alter the culture of the management of people in the firm are
> inherently flawed even when supported by top management.
> (p. 6)
>
> The programmatic approach often falsely assumes that
> attempts to change how people think through mission state-
> ments or training programs will lead to useful changes in how
> people actually behave at work. In contrast our findings sug-
> gest that people learn new patterns through their interaction
> with others on the job. (p. 150)

Stacey (1992) extends these ideas starting with a critique of the
vision-driven model which prescribes the following:

> . . . form a vision of the future state we desire to achieve, per-
> suade others to believe in it as well, and then together, if we get
> our facts right, we will be able to realize it. In this view, top
> management action will take the form of trying to find out in
> advance what is likely to happen. Managers will prepare fore-
> casts, and they will go off for weekends to formulate visions
> and missions. They will mount comprehensive culture change
> programs of persuasion and propaganda to get people through-
> out the organization to commit to a new vision. But if the

belief upon which these actions are based is unfounded, they will have wasted their time and probably missed doing what was really necessary for success. (p. 125)

Further:

Reliance on visions perpetuates cultures of dependence and conformity that obstruct the questioning and complex learning necessary for innovative leadership. (p. 139)

Recall Stacey's advice that 'success has to be the discovery of patterns that emerge through actions we take in response to the changing agendas of issues we identify' (p. 124). Stacey concludes:

The dynamic systems perspective thus leads managers to think in terms, not of the prior intention represented by objectives and visions, but of continuously developing agendas of issues, aspirations, challenges, and individual intentions. The key to emerging strategy is the effectiveness with which managers in an organization build and deal with such agendas of issues.

This perspective produces a different definition of intention in an organization. Instead of intention to secure something relatively known and fixed, it becomes intention to discover what, why, and how to achieve. Such intention arises not from what managers foresee but from what they have experienced and now understand. It is intention to be creative and deal with what comes, not intention to achieve some particular future state. (p. 146)

In short, the critical question is not whether visions are important, but *how* they can be shaped and reshaped given the complexity of change. Visions die prematurely when they are mere paper products churned out by leadership teams, when they are static or even wrong, and when they attempt to impose a false consensus suppressing rather than enabling personal visions to flourish.

And yes, visions can die or fail to develop in the first place if too many people are involved at the beginning, when leaders fail to advocate their views, when superficial talk rather than grounded inquiry and action is the method used. Another paradox. Trying to get everyone on board in advance of action cannot work because it does not connect to the reality of dynamic complexity. Understanding this process puts the concept of ownership in perspective. Ownership cannot be achieved *in advance* of learning something new.

Deep ownership comes through the learning that arises from full engagement in solving problems. In this sense, ownership is stronger in the middle of a successful change process than at the beginning, and stronger still at the end than at the middle or beginning. Ownership is a process as well as a state. Saying that ownership is crucial begs the question, unless one knows how it is achieved.

Strategic planning is also called into question. Spending too much time and energy on advance planning, even if it builds in principles of flexibility, is a mistake. Participation, elaborate needs assessment, formal strategic plans are uncalled for at the outset of complex change processes. Louis and Miles (1990) call this the evolutionary perspective.

> The evolutionary perspective rests on the assumption that the environment both inside and outside organizations is often chaotic. No specific plan can last for very long, because it will either become outmoded due to changing external pressures, or because disagreement over priorities arises within the organization. Yet, there is no reason to assume that the best response is to plan passively, relying on incremental decisions. Instead, the organization can cycle back and forth between efforts to gain normative consensus about what it may become, to plan strategies for getting there, and to carry out decentralized incremental experimentation that harnesses the creativity of all members to the change effort . . . Strategy is viewed as a flexible tool, rather than a semi-permanent expansion of the mission. (p. 193)

The development of authentic shared vision builds on the skills of change agentry: personal vision building through moral purpose, inquiry, mastery, and collaboration (chapter 2). Collective vision-building is a deepening, 'reinforcing process of increasing clarity, enthusiasm, communication and commitment' (Senge, 1990, p. 227). As people talk, try things out, inquire, re-try — all of this jointly — people become more skilled, ideas become clearer, shared commitment gets stronger. *Productive change is very much a process of mobilization and positive contagion.*

'Ready, fire, aim' is the more fruitful sequence if we want to take a linear snapshot of an organization undergoing major reform. Ready is important, there has to be some notion of direction, but it is killing to bog down the process with vision, mission, and strategic planning, before you know enough about dynamic reality. Fire is action and inquiry where skills, clarity, and learning are fostered. Aim is crystallizing new beliefs, formulating mission and vision statements and focussing strategic planning. Vision and strategic planning come later; if anything they come at *step 3*, not step 1.

In working on reform in teacher education in Toronto we have experienced this sequence over the past five years. When we started in 1988 we deliberately rejected launching immediately into large-scale strategic planning, or establishing yet another task force. Instead we began with a few readiness principles: work on the teacher education continuum, link teacher development and school development, commit to some field-based programs, work in partnership with schools, infuse our efforts with continuous inquiry. The firing part took the form of establishing a number of field-based pilot projects with different teams of faculty and cohorts of student teachers, and entering into action-oriented agreements like the Learning Consortium (see chapters 5 and 6). Near the end of year 3 we were ready to focus our aim, by establishing a Strategic Planning Committee and hiring an external consultant to facilitate the process with the Committee and the faculty as a whole. In a faculty-wide retreat with student representatives we generated images of what we should be striving for which were grounded in people's experiences through the pilot projects and other ideas. I believe, we were far more able to be clear (the aim) through this sequence than we would have had we started with the development of (what would have been) an abstract and/or partially owned mission statement and strategic plan. There is still debate and unresolved issues, but we are now in a far better position to pursue reforms with greater clarity of purpose as we enter new phases, driven (this time) by shared vision (see chapter 6).

Thorah Elementary School, north-east of Toronto in our Learning Consortium, is another case in point. Starting on a small scale (the Principal and two teachers out of a staff of twenty-three), the school developed from an individualistic to a highly collaborative culture over a three-year period; not by starting with a vision, but by working toward a shared vision generated through their actions (Fullan, 1992).

Pascale (1990) also captures the ready-fire-aim sequence when he analyzes how the Ford Motor company developed a widely shared mission and values statement in the 1980s.

> In hindsight, a major factor in the wide acceptance of this statement [Ford's vision and values] is that its principles were *enacted* for several years before they were formally announced. Most companies disseminate their value statements the other way around, and the product is dismissed as PR hype. (p. 170)

Charismatic, high flying leaders and premature strategic planning are blinding because they 'distract us from our *own* possibilities' (*ibid*, p. 265). In the new paradigm of change organizations will have to reverse traditionally held assumptions about vision and planning. By so doing they will 'arrive at' deeper and more powerful shared visions which inspire committed action on a day-to-day basis throughout the organization. But 'arrival' as we have seen is only temporary; the most powerful shared visions are those that contain the basis for further generative learning and recognize that individual and organizational development will always be in dynamic tension. Recognizing, indeed valuing this tension, and incorporating values and mechanisms for continually processing it is essential.

Contending with the forces of change is a never-ending process of finding creative ways to struggle with inherently contentious factors — and none more so than Lesson 5.

Lesson 5: Individualism and Collectivism Must Have Equal Power

(There are no one-sided solutions to isolation and groupthink.)

Productive educational change is also a process of overcoming isolation while not succumbing to groupthink. Paradoxes provide the seeds for learning under conditions of dynamic complexity:

> Paradox serves us by setting up polar opposites and affirming both sides. Two factors, mutual exclusivity and simultaneity are essential for a genuine paradox . . .
>
> It is useful to draw a distinction between two types of problems: *convergent* problems (such as balancing your checkbook) that deal with distinct, quantifiable problems amenable to logic, and *divergent* problems (how to reorganize the production department) that are not quantifiable or verifiable, and that do not lend themselves to a single solution. When one solves a convergent problem, one literally eliminates it. There is nothing wrong with that. Divergent problems, however, cannot be permanently eliminated, and benefit from the lateral thinking that paradox evokes. (Pascale, 1990, p. 110)

There are few more endemic paradoxes in humankind than the creative tension between individual and group development. As with all paradoxes there are no one-sided solutions. To illustrate let us trace through the problem of isolation in search of a solution.

Teaching has long been called 'a lonely profession', always in pejorative terms. The professional isolation of teachers limits access to new ideas and better solutions, drives stress inward to fester and accumulate, fails to recognize and praise success, and permits incompetence to exist and persist to the detriment of students, colleagues, and the teachers themselves. Isolation allows, even if it does not always produce, conservatism and resistance to innovation in teaching (Lortie, 1975).

Isolation and privatism have many causes. Often they can seem a kind of personality weakness revealed in competitiveness, defensiveness about criticism, and a tendency to hog resources. But people are creatures of circumstance, and when isolation is widespread, we have to ask what it is about our schools that creates so much of it.

Isolation is a problem because it imposes a ceiling affect on inquiry and learning. Solutions are limited to the experiences of the individual. For complex change you need many people working insightfully on the solution and committing themselves to concentrated action together. In the words of Konosuke Matsushita, founder of Matsushita Electric Ltd.

> Business, we know, is now so complex and difficult, the survival of firms hazardous in an environment increasingly unpredictable, competitive and fraught with danger, that their continued existence depends on the day-to-day mobilization of every ounce of intelligence. (quoted in Pascale, 1990, p. 27)

Educational problems are all the more complex, and collaborative, 'learning enriched' schools do better than those lingering with the isolationist traditions of teaching (Rosenholtz, 1989; Fullan and Hargreaves, 1991). So what do we do? We drive a good idea to extremes. Collaboration is celebrated as automatically good. Participatory site-based management is the answer. Mentoring and peer coaching are a must. Well, yes and no. Pushed to extremes collaboration becomes 'groupthink' — uncritical conformity to the group, unthinking acceptance of the latest solution, suppression of individual dissent (CRM Films, 1991). People can collaborate to do the wrong things, as well as the right things; and by collaborating too closely they can miss danger signals and learning opportunities.

In moving toward greater collaboration we should not lose sight of the 'good side' of individualism. The capacity to think and work independently is essential to educational reform (Fullan and Hargreaves, 1991). The freshest ideas often come from diversity and those marginal to the group. Keeping in touch with our inner voice, personal reflection, and the capacity to be alone are essential under conditions of constant change forces. Solitude also has its place as a strategy for coping with change (Storr, 1988).

> When from our better selves, we have too long
> Been parted by the hurrying world, and droop,
> Sick of its business, its pleasures tired,
> How gracious, how benign, is Solitude
> (Wordsworth, *The Prelude*, cited in Storr, 1988)

Groups are more vulnerable to faddism than are individuals. The suppressing role of groups is clearly portrayed in Doris Lessing's (1986) *Prisons We Choose To Live Inside*.

> People who have experienced a lot of groups, who perhaps have observed their own behaviour, may agree that the hardest thing in the world is to stand out against one's group, a group of one's peers. Many agree that among one's most shameful memories are of saying that black is white because other people are saying it. (p. 51)

Group-suppression or self-suppression of intuition and experiential knowledge is one of the major reasons why bandwagons and ill-conceived innovations flourish (and then inevitably fade, giving change a bad name). It is for this reason that I see the individual as an undervalued source of reform. Lessing puts it this way: 'it is my belief that it is always the individual, in the long run, who will set the tone, provide the real development in society' (p. 71).

The dark side of groupthink is not just a matter of avoiding the dangers of overconformity. Under conditions of dynamic complexity different points of view often anticipate new problems earlier than do like-minded close-knit groups. Pascale elaborates:

> Internal differences can widen the spectrum of an organization's options by generating new points of view, by promoting disequilibrium and adaptation. There is, in fact, a well-known law of cybernetics — the law of requisite variety — which states that for any system to adapt to its external environment,

its internal controls must incorporate variety. If one reduces variety inside, a system is unable to cope with variety outside. The innovative organization must incorporate variety into its internal processes. (p. 14)

Thus, a tight-knit shared culture is not a desirable end-point:

The dynamic systems perspective leads to a view of culture as emergent. What a group comes to share in the way of culture and philosophy emerges from individual personal beliefs through a learning process that builds up over years. And if the learning process is to continue, if a business is to be continually inno-vative, the emphasis should be on questioning the culture, not sharing it. A dynamic systems perspective points to the im-portance of encouraging counter cultures in order to overcome powerful tendencies to conform and share cultures strongly. (Stacey, 1992, p. 145)

Strong sharing and non-sharing cultures are both defective be-cause they have the effect of creating boundaries that are respectively too tight or too loose (Stacey, 1992). Some degree of multiple cultures is essential for questioning the *status quo* in the face of continually changing and contentious issues in the environment. Canon and Honda, for example, hire some managers from other organizations 'for the express purpose of establishing sizable pockets of new cultures' (Stacey, 1992, p. 198).

It is for these reasons that having a healthy respect for individuals and personal visions is a source of renewal in inquiry-oriented organ-izations. When the future is unknown and the environment changing in unpredictable ways, sources of difference are as important as occa-sions of convergence. Because conflict (properly managed) is essential for productive change, i.e., because problems are our friends, the group that perceives conflict as an opportunity to learn something, instead of as something to be avoided or as an occasion to entrench one's posi-tion, is the group that will prosper. You can't have organizational learning without individual learning, and you can't have learning in groups without processing conflict.

However, we can overcompensate for groupthink by glorifying the individual, stressing autonomy, and failing to work on shared visions thereby dispersing energy. We come full circle — isolation is bad, group dominance is worse. Honouring opposites simultaneously — individualism and collegiality — is the critical message.

Lesson 6: Neither Centralization or Decentralization Works

(Both top-down and bottom-up strategies are necessary.)

Centralization errs on the side of overcontrol, decentralization errs towards chaos. We have known for decades that top-down change doesn't work (you can't mandate what matters). Leaders keep trying because they don't see any alternative and they are impatient for results (either for political or moral reasons). Decentralized solutions like site-based management also fail because groups get preoccupied with governance and frequently flounder when left on their own (see chapters 4 and 5, and Fullan, 1991, pp. 200–9). Even when they are successful for short-periods of time, they cannot stay successful unless they pay attention to the centre and vice-versa. Pascale (1990) puts it this way, in examining the Ford case:

> Change flourishes in a 'sandwich'. When there is consensus above, and pressure below, things happen. While there was no operational consensus at the top as to precisely what should be done at Ford, the trips to Japan caused many senior managers to agree that the problems lay in the way the organization worked. This might not have led anywhere, however, were it not for pressures for change coming from the rank and file. (pp. 126 and 128)

Control at the top as many reform-minded leaders have found, is an illusion. No one can control complex organizations from the top. The key question (or more accurately the constant contention) as Senge (1990, p. 287) says is 'how to achieve control without controlling'. He continues:

> While traditional organizations require management systems that control people's behaviour, learning organizations invest in improving the quality of thinking, the capacity for reflection and team learning, and the ability to develop shared visions and shared understandings of complex business issues. It is these capabilities that will allow learning organizations to be both more locally controlled and more well coordinated than their hierarchical predecessors.

Similarly, it is a mistake for local units, even operating under decentralized schemes to ignore the centre (see lesson 7). For example, school and district development must be coordinated. It is possible for individual schools to become highly collaborative despite their districts, but it is not possible for them *to stay* collaborative under these conditions. Personnel moves, transfers, selection and promotion criteria, policy requirements, budget decisions including staff development resources all take their toll on schools if the relationship is not coordinated (see Fullan, in press).

Put differently, the centre and local units *need each other*. You can't get anywhere by swinging from one dominance to another. What is required is a different two-way relationship of pressure, support and continuous negotiation. It amounts to simultaneous top-down bottom-up influence. Individuals and groups who cannot manage this paradox become whipsawed by the cross-cutting forces of change.

Lesson 7: Connection with the Wider Environment is Critical

(The best organizations learn externally as well as internally.)

Many organizations work hard on internal development but fail to keep a proactive learning stance toward the environment. This fatal flaw is as old as evolution. Smith (1984) makes this profound observation:

> For a social entity such as an organization to reflect on itself, it must have a system representing both itself and the context in which it is imbedded. That's where nonequilibrium comes in. A social system that promotes paradox and fosters disequilibrium (i.e., encourages variation and embraces contrary points of view), has a greater chance of knowing itself (as the by-product of continually reexamining its assumptions and juggling its internal tensions). This in turn generates a reasonable likelihood of being aware of the context in which it operates. (p. 289, quoted in Pascale, 1990)

Dynamic complexity means that there is constant action in the environment. For teachers and schools to be effective two things have to happen. First, individual moral purpose must be linked to a larger social good. Teachers still need to focus on making a difference with individual students, but they must also work on school-wide change to create the working conditions that will be most effective in helping all students learn. Teachers must look for opportunities to join forces with others, and must realize that they are part of a larger movement to develop a learning society through their work with students and parents. It is possible, indeed necessary, for teachers to act locally, while conceptualizing their roles on a higher plane.

Second, to prosper, organizations must be actively plugged into their environments responding to and contributing to the issues of the day. They must engage state policies, not necessarily implement them literally, if they are to protect themselves from eventual imposition. But most fundamentally, learning organizations know that expectations and tensions in the environment contain the seeds of future development. There are far more ideas 'out there' than 'in here' (see chapter 5). Successful organizations have many antennae to tap into and to contribute to the demands of change which are constantly churning in the environment. They treat the internal and external milieu with equal respect. Seeing 'our connectedness to the world' and helping others to see it is a moral purpose and teaching/learning opportunity of the highest order.

Lesson 8: Every Person is a Change Agent

(Change is too important to leave to the experts.)

There are two basic reasons why *every person* working in an enterprise committed to making continuous improvements must be change agents with moral purpose. First, as we have seen, since no one person can possibly understand the complexities of change in dynamically complex systems, it follows that we cannot leave the responsibility to others. Second, and more fundamental, the conditions for the new paradigm of change cannot be established by formal leaders working by themselves. Put differently, each and every teacher has the responsibility to help create an organization capable of individual and collective inquiry and continuous renewal, or it will not happen.

Formal leaders in today's society are generated by a system that is operating under the old paradigm. Therefore, they are unlikely to have the conceptions and instincts necessary to bring about radical changes consistent with the new mindset we have been describing in this chapter. Saul (1992) claims that the 'age of reason' has become bastardized, while burying common sense and moral purpose:

The rational advocacy of efficiency more often than not produces inefficiency. It concentrates on how things are done and loses track of why. It measures costs without understanding real costs. This obsession with linear efficiency is one of the causes of our unending economic crisis . . . Worst of all, it is capable of removing from democracy its greatest strength, the ability to act in a non-conventional manner, just as it removes from individuals their strength as nonlinear beings . . . How could a civilization devoted to structure, expertise and answers evolve into other than a coalition of professional groups? How, then, could the individual citizen not be seen as a serious impediment to getting on with business? (Saul, 1992, pp. 582–583)

It is only by individuals taking action to alter their own environments that there is any chance for deep change. The 'system' will not, indeed cannot, do us any favours. If anything, the educational system is killing itself because it is more designed for the *status quo* while facing societal expectations of major reform. If teachers and other educators want to make a difference, and this is what drives the best of them, moral purpose by itself is not good enough. Moral purpose needs an engine, and that engine is individual, skilled change agents pushing for changes around them, intersecting with other like minded individuals and groups to form the critical mass necessary to bring about continuous improvements.

Conclusion

There are exciting, but no comfortable positions in contending with the forces of change because one must always fight against overcontrol on the one hand, and chaos on the other. There is a pattern underlying the eight lessons of dynamic change and it concerns one's ability to work with polar opposites: simultaneously pushing for change while allowing self-learning to unfold; being prepared for a journey of uncertainty; seeing problems as sources of creative resolution; having a vision, but not being blinded by it; valuing the individual and the group; incorporating centralizing and decentralizing forces; being internally cohesive, but externally oriented; and valuing personal change agentry as the route to system change.

What this analysis means is that in the current struggle between state accountability and local autonomy, *both* are right. Success depends on the extent to which each force can willingly contend with if not embrace the other as necessary for productive educational change.

In so doing, learning all eight lessons and recognizing their dynamic interdependency is essential.

The change process is exceedingly complex as one realizes that it is the *combination* of individuals and societal agencies that make a difference. Teachers are major players in creating learning societies, which by definition are complex. Development is 'the continuing improvement in the capacity to grow and to build ever more connections in more varied environments' (Land and Jarman, 1992, p. 30). Internal connections (within oneself, within one's organization) and external connections (to others and to the environment) must co-exist in dynamic interplay.

As the scale of complexity accelerates in post-modern society our ability to synthesize polar opposites where possible, and work with their co-existence where necessary, is absolutely critical to success. One starts with oneself, but by working actively to create learning organizations, both the individual and the group benefit.

Note

1   I am indebted to Matt Miles who has developed several of these lessons (see Fullan and Miles, 1992).

Chapter 4

The School as a Learning Organization

The school is not now a learning organization. Irregular waves of change, episodic projects, fragmentation of effort, and grinding overload is the lot of most schools. The vast majority of change efforts are misconceived because they fail to understand and harness the combined forces of moral purpose and skilled change agentry. Let us take a closer look — at the student, at why recent reform efforts are failing, at what can be learned from partial success, and at what remains to be done in the new work of the principal and of the teacher in order to transform the school from a bureaucratic organization to a thriving community of learners.

The Child and Education

The problem of course is bigger than the school, and this is why the alliances and partnerships taken up in chapter 5 are essential. The learning organization must be dynamically plugged into its environment if it is to have any chance at all of surviving. What is the school facing, and what are the new goals of education for children in a learning society?

Hodgkinson (1991) paints a startling picture of the extent of the problem in the United States.

> One-third of preschool children are destined for school failure because of poverty, neglect, sickness, handicapping conditions and lack of adult protection and nurturance. (p. 10)

Almost one quarter (23 per cent) of children (birth to age 5) live in poverty; more than 80 per cent of America's one million prisoners are high school dropouts (*ibid*).

The Canadian Institute of Advanced Research (CIAR) in its Human Development Project is building on research that demonstrates that 'there is extensive two-way communication between the neural and immune systems that is modified . . . by the quality of life circumstances and experiences' (CIAR, 1992, p. 1). In particular, differences in early development may predispose children to possess more or less effective coping skills later in life — poor self-esteem, low cognitive competence, inability to cope with stress, difficulty in forming relationships in personal and in work situations. Indeed, there is growing evidence that the quality of relationships experienced by children and youth has significant consequences for mental and physical health in adulthood (*ibid*). In the same vein, Offord, Boyle and Racine (1991) report that over 18 per cent of children 4–16 years of age in Ontario, Canada suffer from one or more psychiatric disorders. They observe that 'children with child mental health problems not only suffer from troublesome symptoms and behaviors, but they experience associated impairment (such as) difficulty in social relationships and in accomplishing satisfactorily in school' (p. 17). And, 'the onset of childhood difficulties can . . . herald a lifetime of serious psychosocial problems' (*ibid*).

Schools obviously cannot solve the problems alone, but they must see themselves as part of the solution. Some recent developments in reexamining and experimenting with the purposes and goals of schools are instructive. Gardner (1991) provides the most comprehensive treatment in *The Unschooled Mind*. He states succinctly what he sees as the basic goal of education: to reach the broadest number of students in developing 'education for understanding', by which he means:

> A sufficient grasp of concepts, principles, or skills so that one can bring them to bear on new problems and situations, deciding in which ways one's present competencies can suffice and in which ways one may require new skills or knowledge. (p. 18)

Gardner presents overwhelming evidence that the modern school is ill-matched to the development of the habits and skills of continuous learning on the part of students. Gardner stresses that much of the curriculum material presented 'strikes many students as alien, if not pointless' (p. 149). He proceeds to document how the current curriculum in reading and literacy, sciences, social science, humanities and the arts — the whole spectrum — fails to address students' misconceptions of subject matter, thereby fundamentally failing to provide 'education for understanding'.

Similarly, Sizer's Coalition of Essential Schools, and his proposed scenario for *Horace's School* of the future is about helping each student to 'learn to use one's mind well' (Sizer, 1992, p. 60). A large number of schools in the US have joined the network; each are attempting to restructure based on the Coalitions' nine essential principles (see also Prestine, in press; and Wasley, 1991). As with Gardner, the ability to use knowledge for problem-solving in real situations is essential. 'Exhibitions' of completed work is the central vehicle for learning and for demonstrating understanding as in the following hypothetical example:

Your group of five classmates is to complete accurately the federal Internal Revenue Service Form 1040 for each of five families. Each member of your group will prepare the 1040 for one of the families. You may work in concert, helping one another. 'Your' particular family's form must be completed by you personally, however.

Attached are complete financial records for the family assigned to you, including the return filed by that family last year. In addition, you will find a blank copy of the current 1040, including related schedules, and explanatory material provided by the Internal Revenue Service.

You will have a month to complete this work. Your result will be 'audited' by an outside expert and one of your classmates after you turn it in. You will have to explain the financial situation of 'your' family and to defend the 1040 return for it which you have presented.

Each of you will serve as 'co-auditor' on the return filed by a student from another group. You will be asked to comment on that return.

Good Luck. Getting your tax amount wrong — or the tax for any of the five families in your group — could end you in legal soup! (Sizer, 1992, p. 48)

The development of a sense of community and the habits and skills of collaboration among students is also a central tenet of all proposals to develop schools as learning organizations from Gardner's 'apprenticeships' and 'children's museums' to Sizer's maxim that teams of teachers should have direct responsibilities for developing a community of learners with given groups of students. Effective learning mirrors effective living:

> The real world demands collaboration, the collective solving of problems . . . Learning to get along, to function effectively in a group, is essential. Evidence and experience also strongly suggest that an individual's personal learning is enhanced by collaborative effort. The act of sharing ideas, of having to put one's own views clearly to others, of finding defensible compromises and conclusions, is in itself educative. (*ibid*, p. 89; see also Schrage, 1990)

Even something as straightforward as the three 'employability skills' recently released by The Conference Board of Canada mirrors well these directions. All companies, they say, need:

- people who can *communicate, think* and *continue to learn* throughout their lives;
- people who can demonstrate *positive attitudes and behaviors, responsibility and adaptability*; and
- people who can *work with others*. (McLaughlin, 1992, p. 3)

Finally, Sarason (1990) talks about an 'overarching goal for students':

> Should not our aim be to judge whatever we do for our children in our schools by the criterion of how we are fostering the desire to continue to learn about self, others, and the world, to live in the world of ideas and possibilities, to see the life span as an endless intellectual and personal quest for knowledge and meaning? (p. 163)

There are three profound conclusions that we can draw from this brief foray into the purpose of education for students. The first is the formidable complexity of the challenge. It is complex at the level of pedagogical substance — figuring out effective approaches for creating and assessing learning under conditions of diversity and constant change. Under these conditions — dynamic complexity if you will — teaching is intrinsically and perennially an uncertain profession (Cohen and Spillane, 1992; McDonald, 1992). It is ever more complex at the level of the politics of reform; here, the conflicts, disagreements, and sheer logistics of the interpersonal and interconstituency actions required for improvement are mind-boggling.

Second, we are facing a *societal* problem with two parts: schools that are ineffective as learning organizations, and agencies and institutions outside the school (families, social agencies, business organizations, higher education institutions, governments) that are also ineffective (see Goodlad, 1992). This is less laying blame everywhere than it is a recognition of the enormity of the problem — it is literally not solvable — and a realization that alliances and partnerships beyond the school are vital if we are to have any chance of making substantial progress (see chapter 5).

Third, and unfortunately not obvious to many of those trying to bring about educational reform: you cannot have students as continuous learners and effective collaborators, without teachers having these same characteristics (Sarason, 1990). This is not a matter of teachers having more enjoyable jobs. It is simply not possible to realize the moral purpose of teaching — making a difference in the lives of students — without similar developments in teachers. Moreover, many of the new goals of education for students — having a sense of purpose, habits of and skills of inquiry, ability to work with others, and to deal with change — are precisely the skills of change agentry. In post-modern society the latter is both a means and an end of education as long as it is coupled with moral purpose. Teachers must succeed if students are to succeed, and students must succeed if society is to succeed.

Why Reform Efforts are Failing

There are two basic reasons why educational reform is failing. One is that the problems are complex and intractable. Workable, powerful solutions are hard to conceive and even harder to put into practice. The other reason is that the strategies that are used do not focus on things that will really make a difference. They fail to address fundamental instructional reform and associated development of new collaborative cultures among educators.

One of the most dramatic examples of the problem is the New Futures Initiative to restructure urban schools in the US funded by the Anne E. Casey Foundation (Wehlage, Smith and Lipman, 1992). Here is what the initiative has going for it:

- The Foundation allocated $40 million over five years as well as technical assistance beyond the grant to four medium-sized cities with 'the aim of substantially altering the life and chances of at-risk youth' (p. 55). The four communities selected were Dayton, Ohio; Little Rock, Arkansas; Pittsburgh, Pennsylvania; and Savannah, Georgia.

- The selected communities were required to establish a collaborative involving families, schools, businesses, social services, and city government. The collaborative was 'to coordinate community plans on behalf of at-risk youth'. (p. 55)
- Each of the four communities was funded to develop a baseline study on the adequacy of existing school and social services.
- Each city was to develop a case management system that would perform three functions: '(a) provide some of the most at-risk youth with a caring adult who could offer support during the middle schools years, if not longer; (b) provide access to an array of services from agencies within the community; and (c) provide the collaborative with a continuous flow of information on the problems of youth and the institutions serving them'. (p. 56)
- Each city 'was required to develop a management information system (MIS) that measured the status of students on ten outcomes' (p. 56) including achievement, attendance, dropouts, youth employment, etc.

Moreover, the Foundation took an active role in providing guidelines and technical assistance on an ongoing basis. The Foundation's own guide stated the challenge in the following words:

The development of the New Futures Collaborative is seen as a long-term, incremental process leading to a significant set of changes in the way in which institutions define the problems of at-risk youth, plan services for them, receive funding, and relate to one another. It is an ambitious agenda, unprecedented in its scope and complexity. (cited in Wehlage *et al*, 1992, p. 56)

Five 'long-term structural reforms' were identified:

(i) Restructuring should result in increased autonomy at the school building level, site-based management, and teacher empowerment that would free educators from centralized bureaucracies and their stifling effects.

(ii) Teachers needed greater flexibility in scheduling and group-
ing students in order to create positive environments and
innovative curricula that promote achievement for at-risk
students.

(iii) Restructuring was to make schools more responsive to
students through various forms of individualization and the
elimination of 'slow' and 'fast' tracks. In addition, schools
were encouraged to find incentives that would lead to greater
academic success for those now in lower tracks.

(iv) To support teachers in their efforts with at-risk students,
schools needed to offer extensive training or staff development activities.

(v) Consistent with the overall rationale of New Futures, schools
were urged to find ways of collaborating and coordinating
with other organizations and agencies, both public and
private, in an effort to multiply the potential of existing
resources.

Wehlage *et al* (1992) report on the extent to which New Futures
was successful in bringing about the kinds of changes attempted during
the first three years (1988–1991) of the five-year initiative. The particular activities varied by city according to local plans. In Dayton for
example, the two schools involved were restructured into clusters of
students and teachers, with a daily advisory and counselling period for
students, extended-day activities, incentives to reward student performance, 'beyond the basics' curriculum and interdisciplinary units, a
common daily planning for teachers, and case managers for all students.

While acknowledging that it is an interim report three years into
the project, Wehlage *et al* draw the following conclusion:

Despite the perception that New Futures was introducing fundamental changes and despite the very high level of effort that
went into these changes, we found that the great majority of
New Futures interventions were not bringing about fundamental
change. Instead they can be described as supplemental in
nature, i.e., they left the basic policies and practices of school
unchanged. (p. 66)

For example, of the twenty-three program components compris-
ing the changes across the four cities, sixteen were classified as having
'no impact' on instruction, five had 'minimal', one had 'some' and one
had 'substantial'. In the authors' words: 'New Futures did not produce

promising changes in the substantive content that students learn. It stimulated almost no fundamental change in the primary intellectual activities . . . in schools' (p. 73).

Nor did the structural changes attempted result in qualitative changes in the working relationships among teachers (let alone between teachers and outside social agencies):

> Teachers were uncertain about how best to use increased opportunities for collaboration. Most were accustomed to working as individuals in separate classrooms and had little or no experience within the school of cooperating with others on group projects. Simply providing time to meet . . . was no guarantee that teachers would know how to work together in ways likely to result in more engaging curriculum and improved student performance. (Wehlage *et al* 1992, p. 76)

My intention is not to single out this initiative. It is impressive in its ambitiousness, and exemplary in its commitment to ongoing evaluation and feedback; and it still may accomplish something substantial given corrective action underway. But there are two confirming lessons contained in the story so far. First, it is not that easy to accomplish fundamental change even with large resources, commitments from a variety of essential partners, and even by focussing on a small number of schools (two in Dayton, four in Little Rock, two in Pittsburgh, and three in Savannah). Note also that this initiative had a good deal of voluntarism, and considerable flexibility in working out the nature of the reform. It was not a case of an externally imposed state or national curriculum, which as we shall see later fares even worse, if it does not attend to the development of new learning and new roles for teachers.

Second, the hardest core to crack is the learning core — changes in instructional practices and in the culture of teaching toward greater collaborative relationships among students, teachers and other potential partners. Stated differently, *to restructure is not to reculture* — a lesson increasingly echoed in other attempts at reform. Changing formal structures is not the same as changing norms, habits, skills and beliefs.

Taylor and Teddlie (1992) draw similar conclusions in their study of the extent of classroom change in 'a district widely acclaimed as a model of restructuring' (p. 4). They examined classrooms in thirty-three schools (sixteen from pilot schools that had established school-based management (SBM) programs and seventeen from non-pilot schools in the same district). Taylor and Teddlie did find that teachers in the pilot schools reported higher levels of participation in decision making, but they found *no* differences in teaching strategies used (teacher-directed, low student involvement in both sets of cases dominated). Further, there was little evidence of teacher-teacher collaboration. Extensive collaboration was reported in only two of the thirty-three schools and both were from non-pilot schools. Taylor and Teddlie observe:

> Teachers in this study did not alter their practice . . . increasing their participation in decision-making did not overcome norms of autonomy so that teachers would feel empowered to collaborate with their colleagues. (p. 10)

Other evidence from classroom observation failed to indicate changes in classroom environment and student learning activities. Despite considerable rhetoric and what the authors saw as 'a genuine desire to professionalize teaching', 'the core mission of the school seemed ancillary to the SBM project' (p. 19). Again substantive changes in pedagogy (teaching strategies and assessment), and in the way teachers worked together on instructional matters proved to be elusive. These findings would not be as noteworthy, claim the authors, except for the fact that 'the study occurred in a district recognized nationally as a leader in implementing restructuring reforms' (p. 16). Similarly, Hallinger, Murphy and Hausman (1991) found that teachers and principals in their sample were highly in favor of restructuring, but did not make connections 'between new governance structures and the teaching-learning process'.

Virtually identical findings arise in Weiss' (1992) investigation of shared decision-making (SDM) in twelve high schools in eleven states in the US (half were selected because they had implemented SDM; the other half were run in a traditional principal-led manner). Weiss did find that teachers in SDM schools were more likely to mention involvement in the decision-making process (i.e., composition of committees, procedures, etc.) but:

> Schools with SDM did not pay more attention to issues of curriculum than traditionally managed schools, and pedagogical issues and student concerns were low on the list for both sets of schools. (p. 2)

Similar findings were obtained in the implementation of the Chicago Reform Act of 1989. In essence this legislation shifted responsibility from the Central Board of Education to Local School Councils (LSCs) for each of the city's 540 public schools, and mandated that each school develop School Improvement Plans (SIPs). The LSCs by law consist of eleven or twelve members (six parents, two teachers, two community representatives, the school principal — and in the case of high schools a student). Easton (1991, p. 41) reports that the majority of elementary teachers said that 'their instructional practices had not changed as a result of school reform and will not change as a result of SIP'.

The point is not that participation in decision-making is a bad thing; it is that it is not focussing on the right things — the cultural core of curriculum and instruction.

I hope the point is not lost that I have deliberately selected examples where teachers and others at the local level had considerable leeway and potential to shape the nature of change. It should, but doesn't go without saying that top-down reform strategies have virtually no chance of reaching the core problems. Top-down reforms do have an implicit theory about how to achieve change characterized succinctly by Sarason (1990). Their implicit (and flawed) theory is that:

> Change can come about by proclaiming new policies, or by legislation, or by new performance standards, or by creating a shape-up or ship-out ambience, or all of the preceding. (p. 123)

These 'faulty maps of change' are prevalent in both top-down and bottom-up theories (Fullan and Miles, 1992). Corbett and Wilson's (1990) study of the impact of statewide testing identified several unintended consequences including the diversion of attention and energy from more basic reforms in the structure and practice of schools, and reduced teacher motivation, morale, and collegial interaction necessary to bring about reform. They conclude: 'when the modal response to statewide testing by professional educators is typified by practices that even the educators acknowledge are counterproductive to improving learning over the long term, then the issue is a "policymaking problem"' (p. 321) (see also Shepard, 1991; and Wise, 1988).

Typical also is the problem of 'add-onitis' or 'projectitis' where the latest interesting innovation is taken on without either a careful assessment of its strengths and weaknesses, or of how or whether it can be integrated with what is already going on. Baker, Curtis and Benenson (1991) provide an illustration:

> A superintendent attends a national meeting where Madeline Hunter gives a speech. He comes back convinced that she can

solve the district's instructional problems and promptly arranges for everyone to be trained in the Hunter method of teaching. When teachers learn more about Hunter's 'scientific' methods and want to dispute her philosophic or pedagogical assumptions, the innovators and administrators in charge of improvement dismiss these concerns as 'unscientific'. The thoughtful teachers who raised questions are labeled as 'resisters' and their attitude as 'uncooperative'. Instead of a dialogue in the school on the prospects of improved teaching, the Hunter plan for improvement becomes the occasion to fragment teachers into at least three groups: the believers, the resisters, and those who are still unsure. The superintendent does not seem to worry about minor problems of faculty fragmentation. He is pleased by his efforts to provide a concrete plan that the school board can understand. (p. 12)

Baker *et al* conclude:

Planned change for these teachers is not the cumulative development of a comprehensive strategy. Rather, it is 'one damned thing after another'. Planned change becomes the preoccupation of the administrators who continue to try to fix the system. For teachers, change becomes a matter of coping with management's penchant for educational fads. (p. 13)

We have already seen that site-based or school-based planning — purportedly intended to combat *ad hoc* innovations — does not serve this purpose, at least in its present form. Another clear example of the difficulty of local planning situated in a national context comes from the work of researchers at the University of Bristol, UK. Wallace (1991) reports on initiatives of local education authorities (LEAs) who mandated local development plans for each school. Wallace studied two primary and two secondary schools as they attempted annual 'development plans' required by their LEA in the context of a National Curriculum, and related initiatives such as in-service training grants from the Department of Education and Science (DES) (now Department for Education (DFE)):

The stated rationale for introducing development plans was, first, to assist schools in coordinating their work following central government reforms and LEA initiatives; second, to provide a focus for the various parties at school and LEA levels with a stake in school development; third, to offer a framework within which support staff from the LEA and higher education institutions could work; and fourth, to respond to the DES requirement that payment of the inservice training grant was conditional on schools formulating a National Curriculum development plan within the framework of whole-school policies. Thus the development plan, while designed as a tool to support schools, was at the same time a response to central government demands that each school must have a plan for implementing the National Curriculum and that LEAs must fulfil their responsibility for staff development and training. (Wallace, 1991, p. 392)

In brief, Wallace found that the required developmental planning process did not match the realities and complexities of the school. He concludes:

The development plan represented additional work which proved to have limited value in supporting planning in the four schools. Their response was to comply while continuing to rely on less formal planning processes which enabled heads to lead the process of seeking and using room to manoeuvre to implement external innovations in line with their beliefs and values and those of their supporters. The co-existence of the development plan and these less formal planning processes did not result in conflict. The activities of completing the LEA development plan and flexible planning were relatively independent of each other.

With the decline of LEAs in the UK in favor of a national policy mandating the Local Management of Schools (LMS) the critical role and difficulties in school-based developmental planning will become even more acute.

Further work by the Bristol team in three schools elaborates on some of the problems (McMahon and Wallace, 1992). In one case for example, the head of the school and her staff were convinced of the value of developmental planning and experienced in using the process. They developed a framework for activities to which they were firmly committed. Despite this a number of unanticipated developments — internal (e.g. staff turnover) as well as external (e.g. changes or delays in government policies) to the school — forced the staff to take action not envisaged in the plan.

Change in other words is not only complex, but unanticipated events are a normal part of the scene (see chapter 3).

Finally, a study by Berends (1992) of 123 nationally nominated restructured schools in the US revealed that only twenty-eight (23 per cent) had actually comprehensively addressed the four critical components of: student experiences, professional life of teachers, governance, and community coordination.

Berends concludes:

Because the criteria for comprehensive restructuring used here can be considered to be minimal and because the percentage of comprehensively restructured schools is based on a sample of *nominated* schools, the fact that twenty-eight schools appeared to be comprehensively restructured may reflect the infrequency of school restructuring. (pp. 11–12)

I draw several conclusions about the failure to reform:

- Highly visible reform projects, notwithstanding, the evidence of substantial change up-close is slim. Indeed, being in the limelight of change may bear no resemblance to substantial enduring reform. Put another way, projects with less fanfare may be doing more.
- The core culture of teaching and learning is extremely difficult to change, partly because the problems are intractable, and partly because most strategies fail to focus on teaching and learning.
- Change in teaching for more effective learning requires major transformation in the culture of the school, and in the relationship of the school to other agencies — an incredibly complex undertaking.
- Unanticipated changes in the course of any plan or project are guaranteed. They are not abnormal intrusions but part and parcel of the dynamic complexity of present society.

The consequences of this situation relative to the moral purpose of teaching is perversely damaging. There is considerable evidence that good teachers with moral purpose become victims of either cynicism or burnout. While there are no doubt poor teachers who should not be in the profession, the long-term solution involves attracting and retaining teachers who have the dispositions and working circumstances to make a difference in the lives of children (see chapter 6).

In an extensive treatment of research on burnout and stress in

American teachers, Farber (1991) examines the killing affect of persistent pressure and frustration. The concept of burnout has a number of different meanings in the literature but it includes notions of 'highly motivated workers who react to stress by overworking until they collapse' and 'the discrepancy between a worker's input (what he or she invests in the job) and output (feelings of satisfaction and gratification derived from the work' (Farber, 1991, p. 2). Farber, citing extensive other research, questions whether the typical pattern of burnout arises from frustrated overcommitment. It is more likely he argues that continuous inability to make a difference leads to withdrawal of energy and 'a loss of commitment and moral purpose in work' (Cherniss and Krantz, 1983, quoted in Farber, 1991, p. 17). Farber (1991) in a hypothetical profile of Rachel B., a highly motivated new teacher, describes how such burnout might play itself out:

> She was surprised at first at how difficult it was to teach — there were so many distractions, classroom interruptions, behavior problems, and administrative requests. She had majored in education and spent two semesters in a classroom as a student teacher, and so she didn't expect to feel unprepared or inadequate. She did feel competent in preparing lessons and working directly with the children but felt as if she had very little sense of how to organize a classroom — her experience was in working in classrooms that were already functioning and well established. Moreover, she felt entirely unskilled in terms of dealing with the adults around her — no one had taught her how to deal effectively with administrators nor how to talk to parents. Her supervisor was not particularly interested in discussing these 'political issues' but preferred instead to focus on lesson plans, curriculum ideas, and classroom design (bulletin boards, seating plans, decoration). She felt that all his advice was well intentioned and that much of it, in fact, was quite helpful. What was discouraging, though, was the constant sense of intrusion into her classroom: the supervisor going over her lesson plans, the administration deciding on the books she was to use, the principal's decision on how her children were to walk down the halls of the school, the new kids who were assigned to her already overcrowded classroom, the monitors coming in with notices and announcements several times a day, the incessant forms she was required to fill out. Somehow she was oblivious to these aspects of a teacher's work while she was student teaching.

Another phenomenon she had been oblivious to was the limited time available to her to get to know other teachers. Over time, she became acquainted with them all, of course, and liked many of them; in turn, she felt as if she gained their respect as a caring, motivated, well-prepared teacher. But during the school day the only real opportunities to socialize, or learn from others, were during her 'prep' (preparation period) and during lunch. Like most other teachers in her school, she ended up spending her prep period by herself, often in her classroom, either preparing lessons or filling out some form or another. And while lunch was pleasant and friendly, again it didn't meet her needs or expectations of a community of mutually supportive professionals. Even dismissal surprised her a bit — she hadn't realized how many teachers were as anxious as most of the children to leave the school immediately after 3.

Initially, she responded to these surprises and disappointments by taking solace in the fact that her work, at least the actual classroom work with the students, was gratifying and challenging. Unfortunately, by the end of her first year, these feelings began to erode. Students she first saw as challenging she now perceived as threatening and resistant; gratifications seemed greatly outweighed by disappointments and frustrations. Lesson plans, once seen as an opportunity to be creative, now became an oppressive, routinized, only marginally useful task. She felt that both her students and administration had taken advantage of her good nature and willingness to give. The 'good' kids in her class — and there were many — appreciated and liked her, but it wasn't enough; overall, she felt unappreciated by too many of the kids and virtually all the parents. Although the administration seemed to like her work, she felt she was being paid lip service; she was appreciated by them because she was a hard-working teacher who didn't cause them any trouble. Even her friends and family generally failed to appreciate how difficult teaching was and how much it took out of her to do a good job.

She began withdrawing from the work — giving less, planning less, and feeling less as if she could make a difference. The more she withdrew, the fewer gratifications she derived from the work, the few moments there were of feeling fulfilled as a teacher. And though intellectually she knew that as her investment in the work decreased so would the satisfactions, she was willing to pay the price and forgo additional rewards.

During her second year, these feelings turned to despair, and she began to disparage the children as well as herself for having decided to become a teacher. Despite finding other sources of satisfaction in her life, she could no longer tolerate waking up each morning to face another day at school. She made up her mind to leave teaching but to try to stay in education at some administrative level. Even this decision, though, was fraught with self-deprecation. She wished she could leave education entirely but felt that she had no other marketable skills or ability. (pp. 17–19)

The current high profile of education is a two-edged sword. On the one hand, higher expectations on the part of society and on the part of teachers and administrators who are in the center of reform projects can generate great initial enthusiasm and commitment. On the other hand, high expectation without the capacity and ideas for subsequent fulfillment is a perfect recipe for burnout. One of the common assumptions of all views of burnout is triggered by feelings of 'inconsequentiality':

a sense on the part of professionals that their efforts to help others have been ineffective, that the task is endless, and that the personal payoffs for their work (in terms of accomplishment, recognition, advancement, or appreciation) have not been forthcoming. (p. 25)

Farber summarizes the process of burnout as follows:

  (i) enthusiasm and dedication give way to
 (ii) frustration and anger in response to personal, work-related, and societal stressors, which, in turn, engender
(iii) a sense of inconsequentiality, which leads to
 (iv) withdrawal of commitment and then to
  (v) increased personal vulnerability with multiple physical (headaches, hypertension, and so on), cognitive ('they're to blame'; 'I need to take care of myself'), and emotional (irritability, sadness) symptoms, which, unless dealt with,
 (vi) escalate until a sense of depletion and loss of caring occurs. (p. 35)

The syndrome is perverse because many teachers: 'begin their work with enthusiasm and dedication, with a sense that their work is socially meaningful and will yield great personal satisfactions' which dissipates as 'the inevitable difficulties of teaching . . . interact with personal issues and vulnerabilities, as well as social pressures and values, to engender a sense of frustration and force a reassessment of the possibilities of the job and the investment one wants to make in it' (*ibid*; for a similar portrayal in Canada see Jevine and Zingle, 1992).

Since most attempts at reform are misconceived — failing to address the core of teaching and learning, while coming and going in a superficial, piecemeal, *ad hoc* fashion — they actually make matters worse by discouraging all teachers, but especially those with a greater sense of commitment. Baker *et al* (1991) observe that: 'we often met highly dedicated teachers who were turned off by the new improvement plans. They were convinced that all the bubbly talk about improvement offered little of genuine substance (p. 11).

Hart and Murphy's (1990) study of teachers early in their careers brings the problem into bold relief. They interviewed teachers with five or fewer years of experience concerning their response to the work redesign implications of a career ladder reform being implemented by the district. Teachers in the sample were grouped according to high, medium, and low academic ability and promise (based on a combination of academic average and principal rating of promise). Hart and Murphy's findings are revealing and disturbing. They found that teachers with high promise and ability used different criteria in assessing their work and teaching as an occupation. Specifically, for high promise/ability teachers:

(i) Security was less important compared with professional growth opportunities, access to power and leadership, and a focus on student outcomes. Work structures emphasizing student performance rather than rules and regulations were more important to the high group.

(ii) While teacher empowerment appealed to all groups of new teachers, the high group saw this feature as an opportunity to provide leadership and influence student learning, while the other group saw it in terms of a predictable 'step and lane system' in career terms.

(iii) The low status of the teaching profession and the low esteem in which teachers are held in the community was a source of dissatisfaction for the high group teachers.

(iv) Job satisfaction of the high group teachers was related to clear linkages between work structures, incentives, teaching and learning, and performance outcomes; inequalities in work assignment and reward structures, and make-work projects that only increased earning power were devalued.

(v)   Professional development and growth through leadership and a chance to prove themselves were more attractive to high group teachers, while more formalized supervision, feedback, and in-service appealed to medium and low group new teachers. The low group respondents liked the security of the salary step system through the earning of college credits and other predictable activities.

(vi) High group teachers felt less constrained in their future career opportunities. They were more likely to be unsure about their plans and showed less concern about leaving teaching. They were committed to making a difference, but only if the school was organized to do so. Teachers in the other groups who were dissatisfied were more likely to feel locked into their career choice.

In further explorations, Hart concludes that high ability-high promise teachers are particularly affected by unfulfilling work conditions, and they find that clumsy attempts at improvement add insult to injury.

> When teachers judge their new tasks to be trivial or disconnected from their core teaching tasks . . . they express contempt for new work designs; when they see new tasks contributing to quality instruction and core teaching and learning activities, they praise them. (Hart, 1992, p. 25)

In short, it is only those reform efforts that zero-in on changes in teaching and learning, and the surrounding conditions that support such developments in a sustained way that are likely to fuel and refuel the moral purpose of teaching. Clumsy or superficial attempts at reform, actually decrease commitment — they make matters worse.

What Can be Learned from Partial Success

While there are no resounding successes, and in many ways there is no such thing, given the perennial complexity of change, we can obtain glimpses of a more powerful future by deriving lessons from examples of partial success currently underway. It is my contention that these examples point to the central role of moral purpose and change agentry, and their roles in the learning organization of tomorrow. Three examples are considered: (i) a restructuring project in the state of Maine, US; (ii) a study of restructuring in New York City, US; and (iii) a study of whole school curriculum in primary schools in the UK. In the concluding section of this chapter I introduce several additional examples of success as we consider the new work of principals and teachers (see also the successful examples of partnerships described in chapter 5).

Cox and deFrees (1991) report on work in progress in ten schools in Maine participating in a state-wide restructuring program across primary, middle school, and high schools. These schools have made considerable progress in four areas: refocussing student experiences; altering teaching and learning; redesigning the school; and making connections with people and agencies outside the school. The authors emphasize that there is no single recipe for restructuring, but that there were certain common ingredients across the ten projects:

(i) *Getting Clear on the Focus of Change*

- Building a shared vision of what students should know and be able to do.
- Defining student outcomes that bring the vision to life.
- Distilling and integrating curriculum along with broadening the repertoire of instructional strategies.
- Altering assessment to capture what students know in order to inform the next step.
- Expanding professional development to include learning while doing and learning from doing.

(ii) *Making Change Organizational and Systemic*

- Restructuring is all about time — making time, taking time, finding more meaningful ways to spend time.
- Restructuring means forging initial links to new ideas and new practices, altering the way state and local people work together, the way school people and university people relate to one another, and so on.
- Restructuring provokes questions about power: What does it mean to have young people who can think, teachers who can make decisions, administrators who are effective advocates for learning, and school boards and parents who are active and knowledgeable participants in the education process?

(iii) *Managing the Ongoing Change Process*

- Restructuring means learning to manage and maintain change over time, among many people, and in many areas of action.
- Restructuring is simultaneous, interactive and messy, rather than a tidy and finite sequence of steps.
- Restructuring involves adults in the school and in the community talking to one another and with students about what constitutes learning and then joining forces to make it happen.
- Restructuring around successful learning for all students takes many years and the persistence to make changes, assess results, and modify as necessary.
- Restructuring begets questions faster than they are answered.

(iv) *Deploying State Restructuring Grants Funds to Spur Change*

- Professional development; release time.
- Impetus to organize budgets around student learning.
- Recognition and legitimization.
- Opportunity to analyze and reflect. (pp. 29–36)

Similarly, Lieberman, Darling-Hammond and Zuckerman (1991) describe the early lessons from the 'Schools of Tomorrow . . . Today' (ST/T) project in twelve schools in New York City. Among the positive outcomes in the ST/T schools were:

- Concrete, student-centered changes in curriculum and teaching strategies, expansion of extracurricular activities and special events involving parents and students outside of normal school hours, and the institution of more successful approaches to such aspects of school life as discipline and classroom management.
- The creation of a sense of hope and momentum within the faculty and, often, parent community, as long-standing concerns were aired and initiatives were launched to deal with them.
- The identification and mobilization of previously hidden strengths, talents, and shared ideals among staff who began to seek out more opportunities to work together toward common goals.

- The strengthening of professional norms and institutional capacities for improvement, as faculty learned how to collaborate, deepened their professional expertise, and made time — before and after school hours, in the lunchroom and faculty room, during breaks and prep periods — to talk about ways to improve teaching and learning for students. (Lieberman *et al* 1991, pp. 35–6)

The lessons learned identified by the authors are becoming increasingly familiar in this chapter:

- Conflict is a necessary part of change.
- New behaviors must be learned.
- Team-building must extend to the entire school.
- Process and content are interrelated (interpersonal dynamics and sound ideas must go together).
- Finding time for change enhances the prospects for success.
- A big vision with small building blocks can create consensus and progress.
- Manageable initial projects with wide involvement and visible concrete results sustain the restructuring process.
- Facilitators along with opportunities for training and for retreats, are critical components of successful restructuring efforts. (*ibid*, pp. 36–8)

A study of whole school curriculum development in five primary schools in England allows us to dig deeper into the nature of relationships and the processes involved in coordinating the work of the whole staff (Nias, Southworth and Campbell, 1992).

Primary schools in England tend to be small. The five selected schools ranged in size from six to eleven staff (150–300 students); two were in rural and three in urban settings; none were situated in inner cities. Thus, generalizations should be made with caution. Nonetheless, since the five schools were selected on the basis of their commitment to work as a group, on whole school curriculum development, they offer particularly good examples of the dynamics of collaboration and change.

The themes discussed by Nias and her colleagues confirm as well as shed additional light on the key factors related to continuous improvement. Four themes stand out in Nias' *et al's* investigation: (i) the central importance of teachers' learning, individually and in relation to colleagues; (ii) how changes in teachers' beliefs and practices toward greater 'sharedness' evolve over time and how independence and inter-dependence co-exist in dynamic tension — conflict is normal; (iii) how the working conditions for continuous learning and continuous development of whole school curriculum inhibit or facilitate the process; and (iv) how complexity, unpredictability, and constant shifts internal to the school as well as in the external policy environment are inevitable.

The first and foundation theme identified by Nias *et al* is *teachers' learning*:

> Both teachers and heads saw professional learning as the key to the development of the curriculum and as the main way to improve the quality of children's education. Although they responded during the year to internal and external pressures for change, the main impetus for their learning came from the shared belief that existed in all the schools that practice could always be improved and hence that professional development was a never-ending process, a way of life. (*ibid*, p. 72)

And,

> Teachers who wanted to improve their practice were characterized by four attitudes: they accepted that it was possible to improve, were ready to be self critical, and to recognize better practice than their own within the school or elsewhere, and they were willing to learn what had to be learned in order to be able to do what needed or had to be done. (*ibid*, p. 73)

It is important to note that this personal commitment to learn played itself out in 'a community of learners' in which teacher colleagues and the head continually reinforced the expectation, and conditions conducive to learning. As Nias *et al* observe: 'Seeing colleagues learning was an added encouragement, because individuals realized that they were not alone in their need to learn. Learning was regarded as a means of increasing one's ability, not as a sign of inadequacy; the desire to improve practice also led to a constant quest for "good ideas", that is ideas that were relevant to classroom practice' (*ibid*, p. 76). 'The experience of working together also enabled and encouraged teachers to challenge one another's thinking and practice' (*ibid*, p. 88).

A critical finding was that the climate of support, combined with a commitment to learning together, generated a more, rather than less, questioning approach to improvement, and more rather than less risk-taking:

When such support was available, individuals felt encouraged to take risks, to do something they had perhaps never done before, knowing that whether success or failure followed, they would be able to share the results with their colleagues. (*ibid*, p. 103)

Finally, this commitment to learning was continually reinforced through the actions and expectations of heads:

Habitual learners themselves, these headteachers valued learning, and were willing to contribute to the growth of others, particularly to that of their colleagues. This they did in several ways. They encouraged and actively supported the interests of staff and responded to their concerns by recommending courses, other schools to visit, people to talk to or appropriate reading. They initiated developments themselves and supported the initiatives taken by others. (*ibid*, p. 104)

Second, in the process of working together many *teachers changed their beliefs and practices over time*, but tensions and disagreements had to be worked through for this to occur. As stated by one teacher:

I think each teacher here can contribute their own particular stamp on the school and the curriculum. I don't think we are that dogmatic as a staff that you've got to do things in such a way. Having said that I think if anybody came here who was much happier to shut the door and get on in their own way, completely on their own, they would probably find that difficult because we do quite a lot of things together. They would definitely need to be able to work with other people. (Teacher, Ingham)

I think where the tensions exist you've got to find ways of getting through it. I've learned a lot about myself, as well as other things . . . Life isn't really about . . . being alike and sharing the same attitudes. Tension is part of collaborative working (Teacher, Orchard). (*ibid*, p. 153)

Contrary to currently popular notions these schools did not develop by first engaging in strategic planning, or developing a mission statement, or by formulating a school development plan. A shared sense of purpose, and related concerted action is something to work *toward*, and is never fully achieved.

'Whole schools' are not built on shared intentions, important though these are, but on individuals' efforts to realize through their actions the beliefs and values that they share with their colleagues. Similarly, teachers engage knowledge, but so that they can behave in ways which will increase or enhance their pupils' learning. (*ibid*, p. 154)

And, 'a written statement was produced when it would promote the process of development and not as an end in itself' (*ibid*, p. 167). Nias *et al* present a number of examples of how teachers reexamined their values and beliefs, and acquired or sought the knowledge, skills and attitudes to put beliefs into actions. Whole school curriculum development, the authors, say, 'occurred when a combination of "learning what" and "learning how" resulted in extensions to them both' (*ibid*, p. 166).

Third, Nias *et al* found that there were four key conditions that facilitated whole school curriculum development, namely:

(i)   working toward certain *shared institutional values*, specifically: valuing learning, valuing interdependence and teamwork, valuing the open expression of professional differences, valuing individuals through mutual consideration and support, and valuing a willingness to compromise;

(ii) *organizational structures*: such as decision-making and communication forums, teaching pairs or teams, team projects;

(iii) *resources: commitment, time, people, materials*. Commitment as a resource is an outcome of many of the factors discussed in this chapter. Committed teachers resent spending time on activities that bear little direct relationship to learning, especially innovations and procedures that are destined to go nowhere. Further, when commitment is shared in the service of a greater school-wide purpose, the best teachers do not limit their interests to their own classroom, but also commit to their colleagues, and the development of teaching and learning in the school as a whole. In the latter case, some amount of time must be built into the schedule for teachers to work on these extra classroom developments. Only one of the five schools had managed to establish time for teachers to work together with the regular schedule;

(iv) *leadership* was the fourth condition which influenced whole school curriculum development, not only the key role of heads, but also in the form of a number of teacher leaders who had responsibility for particular projects, and others who took initiatives to support or share with others.

The fourth and final major theme documented by Nias *et al* highlights *the unpredictable and dynamic nature of the change process* as factors beyond the control of the school continually presented themselves.

Initiatives can be overtaken by events elsewhere (for example, legislation) or inhibited by changes in the school (for example, personnel). Either or both of these can have the effect of altering the pace and tempo of development. They can also make school initiatives redundant or adversely affect the staff to such an extent that developments temporarily halt or even regress. (*ibid*, p. 245)

The vicissitudes of policy requirements, in this case arising from the National Curriculum initiatives, provide a constant source of unpredictability, particularly because policy-making in post-modern society is decidedly non-linear (see also Wallace, 1991).

In the end, Nias *et al* conclude that whole school curriculum development, as with other major change, is inherently and persistently complex, that individual and shared concerns must coexist in dynamic tension, and that under these conditions continuous learning — individually and organizationally — is the key ingredient for development. There is no final end point to change.

The New Work of the Principal and the Teacher

Taking the themes of the first four chapters together we now begin to see the challenge of change faced by principals and teachers. There is no question that the work of educators must change dramatically — and change in certain ways — if there is to be any chance of coping effectively and of having education contribute to individual and societal development. We are not yet in a position to know in detail what the most productive forms should be for the future, but we are obtaining clear glimpses of the emerging patterns.

First, because the best pedagogical solutions remain to be developed and worked out, and because these solutions are ever complex and diverse according to different situations, the task is formidable.

Second, because post-modern society is dynamically complex and highly political, the change process, however well planned, will be fraught with unpredictable and uncontrollable problems and opportunities which in turn will generate scores of ramifications. Educational change is inevitably non-linear and unending.

Third, under these conditions having a sense of moral purpose and vision can be decided advantage, but clarity of purpose can also be a liability if the vision is rigid and/or wrong, and if the process of vision-building does not result in a *shared* sense of purpose.

Fourth, the individual and group must co-exist in dynamic tension. No situation that is based either on widespread individual autonomy or on group consensus will be functional. There must be a constant give and take between the individual and the group.

Fifth, because the task is overwhelming, and because different constituencies all see themselves as having a stake in the outcomes, the capacity to enter partnerships and form alliances is essential (chapter 5).

Sixth, for all these reasons conflict and disagreement will plague the process, especially at the early stages of working on a problem.

Seventh, it follows that a spirit of inquiry and continuous learning must characterize the whole enterprise, or else all is lost.

Overall, one can best appreciate the future work of educators, by obtaining a deep understanding of the new mindset that is required for contending with the forces of change as described in chapter 3. As heretical as it sounds, reliance on visions and strong shared cultures contains severe limitations for learning from non-linear change. And, focussing on restructuring prior to working on reculturing puts the cart before the horse.

In studying 'the critical path to corporate renewal' in twenty-six companies, Beer *et al* (1990) concluded the following:

- Change efforts that begin by creating corporate programs to alter the culture or the management of people in the firm are inherently flawed even when supported by top management.
- Formal organizational structure and systems are the last things an organization should change when seeking renewal — not the first, as many managers assume.
- Effective changes in the way an organization manages people do not occur by changing the organization's human resource policies and systems.
- Starting corporate renewal at the very top is a high-risk revitalization strategy not employed by the most successful companies.
- Organizations should start corporate revitalization by targeting small, isolated, peripheral operations, not large, central, core operations.

- It is not essential that top management consistently practice what it preaches in the early stages of renewal, although such action is undoubtedly helpful. (p. 6)

Beer *et al* found that isolated pockets of change reflecting new behaviors, led to new thinking which eventually pushed structures and procedures to change. People learn new patterns of behavior primarily through their interactions with others, not through front-end training designs. Training builds on and extends existing momentum. We found this process very clearly in our work in Brock High School in the Learning Consortium (Durham County Board of Education and Faculty of Education, University of Toronto, 1992 video). Change started in the behavior and culture of teaching and teacher relationships, which in turn spread and led to changes in structure.

This raises the interesting hypothesis that reculturing leads to restructuring more effectively than the reverse. In most restructuring reforms new structures are expected to result in new behaviours and cultures, but mostly fail to do so. There is no doubt a reciprocal relationship between structural and cultural change, but it is much more powerful when teachers and administrators begin working in new ways only to discover that school structures are ill-fitted to the new orientations and must be altered. This is a more productive sequence than the reverse when rapidly implemented new structures create confusion, ambiguity, and conflict ultimately leading to retrenchment.

Stacey (1992) extends these ideas by suggesting that new and different ways of working must become part and parcel of postmodern organizations because they constantly face dynamic change forces. Stacey concludes that developing multiple cultures, and establishing flexible structures and learning teams with degrees of freedom to take risks and learn from open-ended situations are essential, because the future is unknowable:

> . . . the dynamics of nonlinear feedback systems are characterized by a combination of regularity and irregularity, of stability and instability. Systems of this kind develop over time by passing through periods of instability, crisis, or chaos and then spontaneously making choices at critical points, producing new directions and new forms of order. (p. 12)

Further,

> In the group dynamics conducive to complex learning, highly competitive win/lose polarization is absent. The dynamics focus on open questioning and public testing of views and

assertions. People use argument and conflict around issues to move toward periodic consensus and commitment concerning a particular issue, yet consensus and commitment are not the norm. They cannot be if people are searching for new perspectives all the time. A group successfully engaged in complex learning is not dominated by dependence on authority or expert figures ... The group alternates between conflict and consensus, between confusion and clarity. (p. 193)

Regular short-term forms of control through feedback applied by structures, procedures and plans *co-exist* with more open-ended experimentation and learning. The latter is not out of control, but operates in the area of 'bounded instability'. Both interactive learning, and the politics of persuasion and authority exercise forms of control as described by Stacey (1992):

People learning in a group are displaying controlled behavior. Connections run from the discovery by individuals of small changes, anomalies, and ambiguities; to choice arising out of reflection, contention, and dialogue concerning the issues being discovered; to exploratory action; and back to discovery again as the processes of choice and the outcomes of exploratory actions provide further prompts to individual discoveries. Here behavior is constrained partly by individual differences in culture and perceptions and by disagreements that prevent a single view from dominating. Behavior is also partly constrained by the shared views that groups working together come to acquire, yet must constantly question if they are to learn. Constraint, then, is a consequence of the tension between sharing and difference. (p. 165)

And,

People interacting politically are also displaying controlled behavior. Connection runs from discovery as the formation of individual and subunit issues; to choice as the building of support through persuasion and negotiation, the application of power; to action; and back to discovery again as action generates yet other issues. Behavior is constrained by the unequal distribution of power, by the existence of hierarchy, and by the need to sustain sufficient support for views about issues and actions to be taken in regard to them. (p. 166)

What then, does all this mean for the new work of educators?

The New Work of the Principal

A good place to start because it shows so clearly what the solution *is not* is how principals and teachers are portrayed in Hollywood movies (Ayers, 1992; Burbach and Figgins, 1992; Farber, 1991, chapter 6). One of the more famous movies is *Lean on Me*, the 1987 film of real-life principal Joe Clark in his one-man crusade to turn around Eastside High in Patterson, New Jersey. Ayers (1992) portrays Joe Clark in the following way:

> Clark begins his tenure with the famous event that framed his career. He assembles 'every hoodlum, drug dealer, and miscreant' on the stage of the auditorium, and in front of the whole school expels the bunch. 'These people are incorrigible', he shouts above the din. 'You are all expurgated, you are dismissed, you are out of here forever.' He turns to the remaining students: 'Next time it may be you. If you do no better than them it will be you' . . . Joe Clark is at war — 'at war to save 2700 other students'. He's in the trenches fighting mano a mano to save the good ones. (pp. 9–10)

A bullhorn and a baseball bat wielded for the good of the majority is an attention getter, and may do some good in an emergency situation, but it is far from, even counterproductive to, mobilizing more fundamental change. Senge (1990) characterizes the problem precisely:

> Our traditional views of leaders — as special people who set the direction, make the key decisions, and energize the troops — are deeply rooted in an individualistic and nonsystemic world view. Especially in the West, leaders are *heroes* — great men (and occasionally women) who 'rise to the fore' in time of crises. Our prevailing leadership myths are still captured by the image of the captain of the cavalry leading the charge to rescue the settlers from the attacking Indians. So long as such myths prevail, they reinforce a focus on short-term events and charismatic heroes rather than on systemic forces and collective learning. At its heart, the traditional view of leadership is based on assumptions of people's powerlessness, their lack of personal vision and inability to master the forces of change, deficits which can be remedied only by a few great leaders. (p. 340)

By contrast the leader's new work for the future is *building learning organizations*:

The new view of leadership in learning organizations centers on subtler and more important tasks. In a learning organization, leaders are designers, stewards, and teachers. They are responsible for *building organizations* where people continually expand their capabilities to understand complexity, clarify vision, and improve shared mental models — that is, they are responsible for learning. (*ibid*)

Senge sees three key capacities that will be required, ones which map exceedingly well on the complexities of the educational change process described in this chapter: leader as designer, leader as steward, and leader as teacher. As *designers*:

The leaders who fare best are those who continually see themselves as designers not crusaders. Many of the best intentioned efforts to foster new learning disciplines founder because those leading the charge forget the first rule of learning: people learn what they need to learn, not what someone else thinks they need to learn.

In essence, the *leader's task is designing the learning processes* whereby people throughout the organization can deal productively with the critical issues they face, and develop their mastery in the learning disciplines. This is new work for most experienced managers, many of whom rose to the top because of their decision-making and problem-solving skills, not their skills in mentoring, coaching, and helping others learn. (*ibid*, p. 345)

As *stewards*, leaders continually seek and oversee the broader purpose and direction of the organization, but:

In a learning organization, leaders may start by pursuing their own vision, but as they learn to listen carefully to others visions they begin to see that their own personal vision is part of something larger. This does not diminish any leader's sense of responsibility for the vision — if anything it deepens it. (*ibid*, p. 352)

Leader as *teacher* is not about teaching other people one's own vision:

Leaders in learning organizations have the ability to conceptualize their strategic insights so that they become public knowledge, open to challenge and further improvement . . . [Leader as teacher] is about fostering learning for everyone. Such leaders help people throughout the organization develop systemic understandings. Accepting this responsibility is the anti-dote to one of the most common downfalls of otherwise gifted learners — losing their commitment to the truth. (*ibid*, p. 356)

Visions can blind as well as enlighten (Fullan, 1992). Our own action guidelines for 'What's Worth Fighting For in Your School' contain practical advice for the principal committed to building learning schools:

(i)   Understand the Culture of the School
(ii)   Value your Teachers: Promote their Professional Growth
(iii)   Extend What You Value
(iv)   Express What You Value
(v)   Promote Collaboration; Not Cooptation
(vi)   Make Menus, Not Mandates
(vii)   Use Bureaucratic Means to Facilitate, Not to Constrain
(viii)   Connect with the Wider Environment. (For elaboration see Fullan and Hargreaves, 1991; and Fullan, 1988)

We also see rather directly the difficulties and the opportunities as principals experience changes in their own roles in new learning organizations. A case in point is the 'Accelerated Schools' initiative led by Hank Levin of Stanford (Levin, 1988). The Accelerated Schools project involves a set of principles, processes and actions on the part of schools that join the network — schools that have a high concentration of 'at-risk' students: 'Accelerated schools combine relevant curriculum, powerful and diverse instructional techniques, and creative school organization to accelerate the progress of all students' (Christensen, 1992). They commit to three principles: unity of purpose, empowerment coupled with responsibility, building on strengths. The schools also commit to a systematic process to develop shared purpose and action including the establishment of an *Inquiry Process*.

Christensen (1992), in investigating the changing role of the administrator in accelerated schools, found that principals must: learn to keep students as the central focus, share power, foster a risk-taking and inquiry climate and procedures, and take time to interact with students, teachers, community, and help keep the larger vision in the forefront of debate, action, and continuous reassessment.

Prestine (in press) identified similar issues in her study of four schools in Sizer's Coalition network. Where progress was made principals were able to help evolve 'new conceptions of power', link school restructuring to larger 'systemic agreements' in the district, and lead the way in 'willingness to take risks', in which they 'actively participate as coaches, confidants, and catalysts for the change process'.

Further, with the proliferation of teacher leadership roles in the school (mentors, peer coaches, career leaders, staff development and curriculum resource teachers, site-based coordinators, etc.) principals are facing new school-leadership dilemmas and opportunities with teachers (Smylie and Brownlee-Conyers, 1992).

In addition to the difficulties connected to the dramatic increase in sophistication required by this new work (i.e., helping to lead a learning organization in situations of great complexity) there are numerous political fallouts from formal policies mandating school based management. Many of these reform policies, as discussed earlier are failing because of an excessive preoccupation with structure and legalities, and an inability to focus on teaching and learning and supportive collaborative cultures. The principal is frequently caught in the middle. In the Chicago Reform cited earlier in this chapter all incumbent principals were to be reviewed (half the first year, the other half in the second year) by Local School Councils in order to decide whether or not to offer them new four-year contracts. Ford (1992) in a study of fourteen schools found numerous ambiguities and difficulties in the principal's new role including the need 'to work longer hours in an altered environment' (p. 7).

Another dimension of the political complexity of the role relates not only to the state or district mandate to produce collaborative school-based development plans, but also to the constant policy and procedural shifts in government requirements — a phenomenon so clearly described by Wallace (1991) in England.

All in all four conclusions seem warranted. First, neither principals as strong 'unilateral leaders' or principals as 'weak followers' are relevant to the future role of schools as learning organizations (see also Baker *et al*, 1991). Even the collaborative primary heads in the studies conducted by Nias and her colleagues, are too dominant for the development envisaged in the new work of school leaders. Witness, for example:

Headteachers were the significant figures; all other leaders were dependent upon them. They provided their schools with a mission based on their educational beliefs, which in turn, helped to develop or sustain the schools' culture. (Nias *et al*, 1989)

And,

> These heads, like other heads . . . believed that they ought to
> provide the underlying 'vision' of their schools. This was made
> up of the ideals which they held for education in general and
> those which related to 'their' school in particular. Thus each
> head's vision brought together a personal statement of belief
> with the beliefs around which he/she wanted the school to
> cohere and which were to underpin practice throughout it. (Nias
> *et al*, 1992, pp. 114 and 115)

Nias *et al* conclude that the heads 'were central and powerful figures
in 'their' schools and remained in control of developments which took
place within them' (p. 243).

Second, the leadership skills in question require great sophistication. Conceptual clarity is hampered by the widespread use of jargon,
and by the co-existence of superficial and substantive attempts at change
operating under the same labels — restructuring, site-based management, collaborative cultures, transformative leadership, and the like.
Even more problematic is the question of what kinds of experiences
and skill training will develop the kind of leadership we are talking
about. Some helpful, but still incomplete suggestions along these lines
are beginning to appear in the literature (Caldwell and Spinks, 1992;
Daresh and Playko, 1992; Leithwood, 1992; Sergiovanni, 1992). The
new technologies of microworlds, collaboration and virtual reality have
the potential to become quantumly more powerful learning tools in
this regard provided that they are coupled with internships and learning
by doing in innovative settings (Schrage, 1990; Senge, 1990, chapter
17). Moreover, the work examining leadership by women provides
insights into the new work of leaders. Rothschild (1990) concludes that
women's socialization prepares them better to develop and lead such
organizations. Women tend, more than men, to negotiate conflict in
ways that protect ongoing working relationships (as compared to seeing
conflict in win-lose terms), and they tend to value relationships in and
of themselves as part of their commitment to care (rather than seeing
relationships as instrumental to other purposes). Shakeshaft (1987) finds
similar patterns in her studies of women and leadership in school
systems, namely: relationships with others are seen as central, teaching
and learning are major focuses, and building a sense of community is
essential.

Third, and more generally, educational leaders must learn to
influence and coordinate non-linear, dynamically complex, change

processes. The necessary mind-set is embedded in the eight lessons in chapter 3. Stacey (1992) identifies seven steps that leaders should take:

- Developing a new understanding of control
- Designing appropriate uses of power
- Establishing self-organizing learning teams
- Developing multiple cultures
- Taking risks
- Improving group learning skills
- Creating resource slack. (p. 188)

Fourth, if the learning organization really takes hold the principalship as we now know it may disappear. Sergiovanni (1992) talks about 'substitutes for leadership' in the sense that as teachers combine a commitment to moral purpose with a continual pursuit of exemplary practice, 'leadership' becomes built in. Every teacher becomes a leader; or more precisely, the ideals, norms and practices of the groups generate their own press for continued improvement. In a real sense, what gives the contemporary principalship inflated importance is the absence of leadership by everyday teachers.

The New Work of the Teacher

Back to the movies. *Stand and Deliver* is a powerful film. The star is Jaime Escalante, who teaches mathematics at a high school in east Los Angeles in an Hispanic community. Burbach and Figgins (1992) observe:

> More than just a work-to-the-contract teacher, Escalante pushes the dedicated, tough love image to new extremes. He meets with a group of largely Hispanic students after school and on weekends to help them prepare for the advanced placement test in calculus, counseling them to work right through Christmas vacation to accomplish their goal. As a dramatic example of how devoted he is to his students, he puts his own health in jeopardy by returning to his teaching duties only two days following a heart attack. (p. 7)

Says, Ayers (1992): 'Like all the saint-teachers he has no life — he is never learning something new, coaching little league, making art, pursuing political projects. He is sacrificing himself for his students alone' (pp. 11–12).

Farber (1991) puts it this way: 'perhaps most insidiously the message of *Stand and Deliver* seems to be that in order to be considered a good teacher, one must work oneself to death' (p. 183). This, and similar films, observes Farber are 'all too willing to sell out an entire professional group to glorify the exceptional individual among them' (p. 183). Moral purpose gone awry!

Movies either portray teachers as lone impassioned martyrs 'who beat all the odds (incompetent administrators, cynical colleagues, apathetic students) in order to make a difference' (Farber, 1991, p. 183), or as incompetent buffoons (as evidenced by *Teachers* (1984), *Ferris Bueller's Day Off* (1986) and others). Burbach and Figgins conclude that there is 'a long history of portraying teachers as generally passive individuals who exert very little control over their professional lives' (pp. 11–12). In either case, teacher as moral martyr, or teacher as powerless incompetent, *the system never changes*.

So, what of the new work of the teacher in a system that is designed to deal with dynamic complexity on a continuous basis. I referred earlier to Sizer's Coalition of Essential Schools, but we have not considered the nature of the process of change that would be required to get such schools up and running. Prestine's (in press) case study of Broadmoor Junior High School in Pekin, Illinois is instructive in this regard. A school of 460 students, grades seven and eight, Broadmoor joined the Illinois Alliance of Essential Schools in 1988. The 1989/90 school year was designated as a planning year in which considerable inservice and other support was available to aid development of a multi-year plan. It was decided to divide the students and faculty into three 'houses'. Teachers' classrooms would be relocated to facilitate team planning and interdisciplinary teaching. Students in each house would consist of half grade seven and half grade eight. It was decided that the whole school would focus on implementing three of the nine principles in year one (student-as-worker, simple goals, and intellectual focus). The plan was to add three more principles in year two, and the final three in year three.

In a word, all hell broke loose in the first year:

Examination of the 1990–91 school year show that all three of the planned implementations for change ran into severe difficulties and none were satisfactorily implemented. Of the several convulsions and general tumult that shook Broadmoor during this year, the scheduling problems by far was the most consequential and devastating, impacting on all three planned changes . . . It became a year of endless infighting, bickering and bad feelings. (*ibid*, pp. 8–9)

Key to productive processes of change is a mindset that conflict is inevitable, 'the problems contended with were not seen as dead ends, but rather as mis-steps that required correction and provided new knowledge and experience to guide further efforts' (*ibid*, p. 10). Plans were reformulated to focus on organization and governance, curriculum, student assessment and pedagogy. There were six priorities built into the schedule: 'increasing usable instructors' time; personalizing the learning environment; ensuring that every student is known well; ensuring success for all students; creating continuity; and integrating learning across subjects' (*ibid*, p. 13).

In the new plan, the school was divided into four teams of 110–120 students. Each cohort of students is taught by a team of four teachers, and supported by resource teachers. Each 'core team is empowered to make revisions which affect its own curriculum and to flexibly schedule its instructional day as the team sees fit' (p. 14). A common planning time of seventy minutes every day is provided for each team as the students go to physical education and alternating exploratory classes. Extensive curriculum materials and activities were developed or assembled in a summer curriculum project. As Prestine observes:

The flexibility of the schedule and the provision for common planning time allow teachers to work together as they personalize instruction and integrate study across subject areas. The only guideline that had to be followed was that no team decision could affect others in the school without those affected being involved in some manner in the decision making process. (pp. 14–15)

It is still too early to determine how successful the new design will be, but student suspensions have declined, and staff are gaining great satisfaction from seeing how well it works with kids. Says one teacher, 'I have never been more excited about my profession than I am now' (p. 15).

Prestine attributes the new success to several critical factors:

- the way in which administrators and staff persisted in developing 'a conceptual grasp of essential school precepts' through continuous in-service and planning-doing-planning-redoing

- the recognition that structural changes would not be sufficient without 'changes in ideas, beliefs, and attitudes'
- a realization that the kind of change they had undertaken involved great 'sophistication and complexity', and a willingness to examine the interconnectedness of all the parts and to expend the effort needed to address the details of complexity
- 'a flexible process orientation' arising from 'the overwhelming perception that (change) is not only continuous and seamless, but also erratic and differential in impact' (p. 21)
- the 'supportive role of the superintendent' including his efforts in fostering a network of relationships among schools, parents and community and the Board of Education
- 'a systematic application and use of philosophy'.

Two overriding conclusions come from this case. One is how central it is for all staff to work on a shared and deeper understanding of a more comprehensive pedagogical philosophy and its relationship to interconnected school structures and associated activities. The second lesson of change is well stated by Prestine:

> If anything can be gleaned from this one case, it is that restructuring is a collaborative, interactive, and systemic experience situated in a given context. The process is always tenuous and dependent on a host of factors that gain varying degrees of significance and importance across both time and a multi-dimensional, fluctuating context. (*ibid*, p. 24)

Sounds like dynamic complexity! And the process is not transportable. The guidelines in this book will be helpful, indeed essential, but only if each setting is prepared to work through its own complexity.

It is significant as well, that as a result of initial experiences with implementing coalition schools, Sizer has altered his thinking about the pace and nature of change. Sizer originally advocated a more rational developmental approach recommending that schools follow 'a relatively slow and deliberate strategy which would encourage the development of understanding, consensus and ownership' (Prestine, 1992, p. 7). Based on first attempts at implementation Sizer later concluded 'I'm increasingly persuaded that schools that go slow and do a little at a time end up doing so little that they succeed only in upsetting everything without accruing the benefits of change' (quoted in *ibid*, p. 8).

Sizer and the coalition now recommend a more aggressive and comprehensive stance:

In a school, everything important touches everything else of importance. Change one consequential aspect of that school and all others will be affected . . . We are stuck with a school reform game in which any change affects all, where everyone must change if anything is to change. (Sizer, 1991, p. 32)

About the process Sizer says:

To get the needed gains for kids, we adults must expect and endure the pain that comes with ambitious rethinking and redesign of schools. To pretend that serious restructuring can be done without honest confrontation is a cruel illusion. (*ibid*, p. 34)

Recall also our reference earlier in this chapter to Levin's Accelerated Schools initiative. In case studies of two elementary schools McCarthy (1992) investigated how such a redesign affects the work of teachers:

This new model of organization necessitates new ways of doing things in schools and creates an initial period of tremendous role ambiguity and conflict. The empowerment of teachers creates conflicting expectations for behavior. Teachers are suddenly thrust from the relative isolation of their classrooms to the larger world of the school. There is much confusion about what decisions they can and should make. There is also great anxiety on their part about their ability to make them. (p. 3)

The Accelerated Schools Projects, like the Coalition of Essential Schools, increasingly draws specifically on the research literature in the areas of collaboration, school change and staff development in designing training and support activities for individual and networked schools. Using interviews and school and classroom observations McCarthy found that 'the process is working' (p. 9). There is greater cooperative planning for instruction among teachers, and evidence of more active and more effective learning. In the words of teachers:

Our teachers now learn from other teachers. There is a great deal of visiting in classrooms, both formal and informal discussions among teachers.

(It) showed me that I could plan learning activities for my students that were relevant, interesting and hands-on and yet be academically focussed. I have turned around the way I run my classroom and the children are really starting to grow socially and academically.

The collaborative inquiry process involving teachers, administrators and parents in Accelerated Schools according to McCarthy, 'seems to have the potential to make lasting and meaningful changes in the culture of the school, unlike other quick-fix solutions' (p. 14).

We are now in a position to sketch in broad strokes what the new work of the teacher entails. At least seven interlocking components will be required.

First, teachers of the future will make their commitment to moral purpose — making a difference in the lives of children — more prominent, more active, more visible, more problematic. Many teachers have moral purpose now, but they do not conceptualize it that way. They do not give themselves the stature they deserve. They must push moral purpose to the forefront, but along with the other components described below. Otherwise it leads to frustration, burnout, cynicism or moral martyrdom.

Second, teachers must substantially deepen their knowledge of pedagogy. They must continually work on personal vision encompassing both moral purpose and a much more sophisticated knowledge of teaching and learning. Hallinger, Murphy and Hausman (1991) comment on how surprisingly limited were the views of principals and teachers about curriculum and pedagogy. While the educators in their sample strongly favored restructuring, they made few connections to how the schools in question might reorganize curriculum and instruction to meet the needs of students. Lichtenstein, McLaughlin and Knudsen (1992) claim that such professional knowledge is the key to legitimating teacher empowerment and effectiveness. Teachers, they argue, must have and be seen to have (i) knowledge of the professional community; (ii) knowledge of education policy; and (iii) knowledge of subject area. The development of greater professional knowledge and competence is vital given the complexity of the learning problems we have documented in this chapter. One also sees the tremendous and ongoing expansion of pedagogical expertise that is required in the schools or learning settings envisaged by Gardner, Sizer, Levin and the like. One witnesses as well, the excitement, ideas, and energy that are unleashed when teachers do have the opportunity to collaborate in redesigning teaching and learning with outside support.

Third, implied in the previous two components, everyday teachers must be cognizant of the links between moral purpose at the school level and larger issues of education policy and societal development.

Fourth, in addition to being their own person *vis-a-vis* purpose and vision, teachers must work in highly interactive and collaborative ways, avoiding the pitfalls of wasted collegiality, while working productively with other teachers, administrators, parents and business and community agencies.

Fifth, teachers will work in new structures. Ones that cluster students, team teachers, provide common planning time, link to parents and community, and participate in wider networks of learning. A prominent finding of Stevenson and Stigler's (1992) comparative study of educational practices in the United States, Japan, Taiwan, and China was that teachers in Asian countries spend much less time in classroom teaching (with larger class sizes), more time interacting with other teachers, more time preparing for and assessing learning, have a common work room in the school, and generally are in a position to get better and better at teaching.

Sixth, in order to do (and be) the foregoing, teachers (individually and collectively) must develop the habits and skills of continuous inquiry and learning, always seeking new ideas inside and outside their own settings. Principals as main conduits to the outside is a dead model. The reason that the role of the principal has taken on such inflated importance, is related to the limited leadership of the everyday teacher. (This I trust will not be construed as the principal being unimportant.)

Seventh, and above all, teachers must immerse themselves in the mysteries, and highs and lows of the dynamic complexity in the change process — how conflict is inevitable, how vision comes later, how individualism and collectivism co-exist in dynamic tension, how arbitrary disturbances in the environment are par for the course, how you never arrive, and how sometimes things get worse despite your best efforts.

I have frequently stressed that teachers cannot afford to wait for the system to change itself. They must push for the kind of professional culture they want, sometimes in the face of unresponsive principals, communities and school districts, and sometimes taking advantage of the increasing opportunities to engage in substantial reform efforts that both restructure and reculture schools towards continuous learning for all. Teachers cannot and should not do this entirely on their own (see chapter 5), but they must play their own aggressive part in breaking the cycle. Finally, the reason that teachers as *individuals* must develop personal change capacity is that they will inevitably find themselves in different groups over time. There is a limitation to working only on the development of the group one happens to be in. No matter how collaborative that group becomes, it will never last because people come and go. Thus, individuals must acquire and carry with them skills in change agentry as they form and reform relationships over time. If enough people and systems focus on the developments, people will find kindred spirits and supportive organizations as they move through their careers.

Two Words of Caution

Groupthink and *balkanization* are the nemesis of hyper-collaboration. We have already signalled the danger of groupthink in collaborative arrangements (chapter 3). Groupthink is the uncritical acceptance and/ or suppression of dissent in going along with group decisions. Janis (1972) who coined the term, and Tuchman (1984) provide numerous examples of how well-intentioned, well-educated groups throughout the ages 'end up mutually reinforcing their biases all the way to self-destruction' (Schrage, 1990, p. 29).

Collaboration is one of the most misunderstood concepts in the change business. It is not automatically a good thing; it does not mean consensus; it does not mean that major disagreements are verboten; it does not mean that the individual should go along with the crowd. Francis Crick, the Nobel prize winner as co-discoverer of the double helix, once told a BBC interviewer 'politeness is the poison of all good collaboration in science' (quoted in *ibid*, p. 42). Schrage elaborates:

> One of the most persistent myths about collaboration is that it requires consensus. This is emphatically not so. Collaborators constantly bicker and argue. For the most part, these arguments are depersonalized and focus on genuine areas of disagreement. (*ibid*, p. 159)

Superficial agreement not conflict is often the source of faulty decision-making (Harvey, 1989). With all the educational bandwagons, and all the *ad hoc*, piecemeal, attractive innovations, educators are particularly susceptible to groupthink. Agreement, as when the staff goes along with a proposal from the administration, or even when the majority of a school vote in favor of a given innovative project does not necessarily mean sound judgment. We have seen in the dynamic complexity of major educational change projects that conflict and disagreement are part and parcel of all productive change processes. There is nothing wrong with pursuing promising ideas provisionally. Taking a questioning stance, especially at the early stages of a change initiative is healthy not heretical.

The antidote to groupthink is change agentry at its best. See, for example, the remarkable congruence between the four strategies for avoiding false consensus recommended in a training video, and the concept of the learning organization: open climate, avoid the isolation of the group, assign members the role of critical evaluator, avoid being too directive (CRM Films, 1991).

Balkanization occurs when strong loyalties form within a group with a resultant indifference or even hostility to other groups. This occurs in large schools when subcultures develop thereby inhibiting school-wide initiatives (Fullan and Hargreaves, 1991). Often one thinks of such subcultures as consisting of reactionaries, but innovative subgroups can easily become inward looking. Innovative whole schools, — at first blush seemingly the ideal — can also become balkanized from their surroundings. Whole school innovative cultures can be problematic in at least three respects. First, loyalties may be so intense at the school level they may interfere with broader commitments to the district or society. Second, and this is where groupthink and balkanization feed on each other, intra-group interaction may limit access to, and due consideration of, other ideas in the environment. Third, even highly successful innovative schools cannot be counted on to last, simply because in situations of dynamic complexity *things change*. Therefore, one cannot depend exclusively on the group one happens to be in at a given time. Educators with moral purpose and the skills of change agentry must be prepared to form and reform a variety of relationships across their careers because that will be reality — constant change, sometimes for the better, sometimes for the worse.

The overarching message for educators in this chapter is that in order to improve learning situations that one cares about, it is necessary to become involved in ideas and matters outside the immediate setting — the school in addition to the classroom, the environment in addition to the school — and to do this without losing focus on the core mission of teaching and learning. The learning organization is dynamic inside, but perforce must be highly plugged into its context. Indeed, the individuals in a learning organization must be able to form new learning partnerships again, again, again and again . . . For that to occur one must have a deep appreciation of the relationship between learning organizations and their environments — a case of dynamic complexity if there ever was one.

Chapter 5

The Learning Organization and its Environment

Learning organizations respect their environments because *ideas* are out there, *politics and partners* are out there, and ultimately *we* are all out there. Indeed the phrase 'out there' is a misnomer for the learning individual and the learning organization. Learning organizations neither ignore nor attempt to dominate their environments. Rather, they learn to live with them interactively. Continuous change is built into the relationship because widespread interactions under conditions of dynamic complexity demand constant attention and movement. Change forces are seen as inevitable and essential to learning and growth.

The key message in this chapter is not that one will find better solutions to existing needs by searching the environment (as true and helpful as this is), but that learning organizations are part of a greater complexity that requires a holistic view to survive and develop. Land and Jarman (1992) capture this new mind-set precisely:

> The reality of evolutionary success demonstrates that 'fitness' is not simply about 'adapting to an environment', but rather the continuing improvement in the capacity to grow and build ever more connections in more varied environments (we define growth and evolution as continuously making more extensive and increasingly complex connections inside the growing organism and with the varied outside environments). (p. 30)

In talking about 'reinventing the corporation', John Seely Brown, Vice President of Xerox, observes that 'innovation is everywhere; the problem is learning from it' (Brown, 1991, p. 103). In analyzing the continuous success of the Hanover Insurance Company, Hampden-Turner (1992) states flatly that the company's 'major claim to distinction is its conscious design as a system that intends to learn from its

84

environment more rapidly than its competitors' (p. 23). And Drucker (1992) adds a vital word to Peters and Waterman's famous phrase 'Managing by Walking Around — Outside!'. Drucker stresses that 'for purposes of broadening the horizon, questioning established beliefs and for organized abandonment, it is better to be confronted with diversity and challenge' (p. 350).

Ideas are Out There

There are countless studies now that show that the majority of schools do not seek and process ideas from the outside. But some schools do (although we have no reason to believe that they *sustain* their innovative capacities). Rosenholtz's (1989) depiction of 'stuck' and 'moving' schools in her sample of seventy-eight elementary schools is clear about the difference between non-learning and learning schools. Rosenholtz found that in the thirteen 'moving' schools in her study, teachers learned from each other and from the outside. Most teachers in these schools, even the most experienced, believed that teaching was inherently difficult. They believed that teachers never stopped learning to teach. Since most teachers acknowledged that teaching was difficult, almost everyone recognized they sometimes needed help. Giving and receiving help did not therefore imply incompetence. It was part of the common quest for continuous improvement. Having their colleagues show support and communicating more with them about what they did led these teachers to have more confidence, more certainty about what they trying to achieve and how well they were achieving it.

As Rosenholtz observes, in effective schools, collaboration is linked with norms and with opportunities for continuous improvement and career-long learning: 'It is assumed that improvement in teaching is a collective rather than individual enterprise, and that analysis, evaluation, and experimentation in concert with colleagues are conditions under which teachers improve' (p. 73). As a result, teachers are more likely to trust, value, and legitimize sharing expertise, seeking advice, and giving help both inside and outside the school. They are more likely to become better and better teachers on the job: 'All of this means that it is far easier to learn to teach, and to learn to teach better, in some schools than in others' (p. 104).

Louis and Miles (1990) found that the two high schools that were successful in achieving major reform (of the five they studied) were much better at 'getting and managing resources for change' (p. 239). They sought resources including money, time, ideas, materials, assistance and training, and the like. They were effective at acquiring new resources, as well as reworking existing ones. The link to other components of change agentry is critical here as elsewhere. It is not the sheer level of resource acquisition that counts — the history of failed reform is replete with high-profile efforts that were resource-rich — but how selective resource seeking is linked with vision-building, mastery, and collective effort. For learning organizations, seeking assistance is a sign of intelligence not weakness (*ibid*).

Baker *et al*'s (1991) study of forty-eight school districts in Illinois confirms that internal development and external involvement must go together. Thirteen of the forty-eight districts were classified as engaged in 'systematic improvement' on a sustained basis. It is no accident that all thirteen successful districts were found to be users of external support from regional educational service centers and several other sources. By contrast in all eight cases that had no external support, there was no evidence of school improvement. Time and again we find that seeking external support and training is a sign of vitality. It is the organizations that act self-sufficient, that are going nowhere. And, as we have seen in chapter 4, it is the schools that have their internal acts together who both seek outside support, and know good ideas when they see them.

Carl Glickman's 'League of Professional Schools' represents another convincing case. Glickman, Allen, and Lunsford (1992) report on the development of the twenty-two schools that joined the league in 1990, and the twenty that joined in 1991. Confirming some of our earlier concerns, they found that shared governance was implemented more readily than an instructional focus on reform in teaching and learning. Glickman *et al* then examined differences in implementation with respect to their three core premises of a 'professional school': shared governance, schoolwide instructional focus, and action research (data collection and action). High implementation was defined as implementation of at least two of the premises and a beginning on the third; low implementation as one or no premises implemented. The four main differences between high and low implementation schools were that the former had:

(i)   A tendency to be inclusive and involve all faculty.

(ii)   Ability to work with or (if necessary) around the district in making school based decisions.

(iii)   The use of time for planning, developing and revising as validation of important work.

(iv)   Ability to ask for help and assistance (to call others, to ask help of each other, to visit others, to ask others to come to the school). (pp. 14–15)

Sounds familiar! In his new book, Glickman (in press) extends these ideas in three themes consistent with this book: (i) The Covenant of Teaching and Learning — 'to prepare productive citizens for participation in democracy' (moral purpose); (ii) The Charter: How to Operate — guiding rules of shared governance; and (iii) The Critical Study — continuous inquiry and information infusion from within and without.

We could go on marshalling similar evidence, but it is sufficient to note that *all* the success stories considered in this book are founded on strong ongoing relationships between external support groups and internal teams. From Sizer's Coalition Schools to Comer's School Development Program that I will describe in the next section, a wide network of ideas and practices focused on particular problems and assumptions is seen as essential to getting anywhere. Further confirmation is found in Murphy and Hallinger's (1993) book in which all the examples of 'learning from ongoing efforts' combine internal learning with external alliances. The underlying reason is directly related to the core capacities of change agentry (chapter 2). Whether at the individual or organizational level, vision-building, inquiry, mastery, and collaboration cannot be exercised in small circles. There is a ceiling effect to conceptualizing inspiring visions, to investigating and solving problems, to achieving greater and greater competencies, and to engaging in productive relationships, if one does not connect to varied and large networks of others involved in similar and different pursuits.

This is why we recommend that principals and teachers constantly strive to 'connect with the wider environment'. Our advice to principals, for example, in addition to a number of guidelines for internal school development, included suggestions for extending the circle of ideas and contacts:

First, he or she needs to be involved outside the school, especially in learning activities. Some examples include: participating in peer coaching projects among principals; working with other principals and administrators in the board to improve professional development for principals; visiting other schools outside as well as inside one's board; spending time in the community; finding out about the latest practices as reported in the professional literature and disseminating ideas about one's own school practices through speeches, workshops and/or writing. It will be necessary to be selective, but ongoing involvement outside the school, in some form, is essential for perpetual learning and effectiveness.

Second, principals should help the school deal with the wider environment. Sometimes this will involve contending with the overload of unwanted or unreasonable change. It might involve urging and facilitating a move toward school-based decision-making within the board. Mostly, however, we suggest that the highest priority be placed by the principal on helping teachers widen the contacts with the professional world outside school. Contacts should be made not just with schools doing similar things, but also with schools involved in different activities, even opposites. Contrast is an important prompt for critical self-reflection. Going 'outside the frame' beyond one's normal traditions, is a great source of learning and improvement. (Fullan and Hargreaves, 1991, p. 97)

Access to external ideas and expertise, however, is only the simplest aspect of the learning organization's relationship to its environment. Having a steady pipeline of new ideas will not result in groundbreaking solutions. The real complexities and profound changes are to be found in the politics and potential partners that are also out there.

The Politics and Partners are Out There

It is not that the environment is particularly friendly (especially for schools). In fact, the fundamental point of the new paradigm is that we cannot expect 'the outside' to organize itself to meet our needs. Dynamic change forces can never operate that way.

Politics and potential partners are at every level. I consider several facets of this complexity in the following paragraphs from large scale state policy, to parents and communities, to businesses, teacher unions, and other agencies.

The first lesson of the political environment is to realize that the larger arena of politics is rife with unpredictable shifts and fragmented initiatives. Wallace (1991) describes in painful detail the seemingly arbitrary surprises that accompanied the unfolding of the Education Reform Act and the evolution of the National Curriculum in Great Britain. In essence, states Wallace:

Attempts at comprehensive and coherent planning were constrained by the surprise or ambiguity caused on occasion by information on central government and LEA (Local Education Authority) compulsory innovations which was either inadequate to guide implementation, contradicted earlier information, or was supplied at very short notice before an externally imposed deadline for action. Few of these experiences could have been foreseen by school staff or governors. Instances included:

(a) a delay of several months for the secondary schools in planning history and geography courses, with related implications for future staffing, until it was certain whether pupils could combine these subjects as a GCSE course;

(b) unanticipated delay in the primary schools in planning for English Key Stage Two while awaiting documents from the National Curriculum Council — which failed to arrive until after the relevant section of the Education Reform Act came into force;

(c) loss of momentum in the secondary schools with the LEA's Records of Achievement Initiative (launched by the LEA in response to a central government initiative) after a central government minister announced that the compulsory component of pupils' records would be restricted to the National Curriculum attainment targets they had reached;

(d) the shelving of appraisal interviews, which had been implemented in one primary school with LEA encouragement, after the Secretary of State announced that the introduction of a national framework would be postponed;

(e) frequent problems in planning expenditure within the formula-funded LMS [Local Management of Schools] budget due to revision . . . of provisional arrangements for the transition from the historic funding level, arithmetical mistakes, and the discovery of unforeseen areas of spending. These factors gave rise to the initiation of redundancy proceedings in one secondary school and to the enforced abandonment of two proposed posts in one primary school;

(f) postponement by LEA staff of in-service training . . . prior to introducing the development plan initiative, until just before the deadline for completion of the plan. (pp. 393–4)

This political reality repeats itself all over the world as governments attempt to plan educational reform on state or national scales. Ask any teacher or administrator. There are at least three responses that could be taken. One is to become cynical, and not initiate any change 'until final decisions about these innovations have been made' (*ibid*, p. 395).

A second is to strive to become indifferent to external machinations — a kind of 'this too shall pass' attitude. Acker (1989) describes how two primary schools in England responded to the introduction of the externally imposed National Curriculum. One of these schools had many of the apparent characteristics of collaboration — high participation in decision-making, caring, warmth, humour, camaraderie and gratitude. As well as the usually mentioned upsides to this culture of collaboration, Acker's study identified a number of difficulties. This school, despite being collaborative internally, was not well connected to the environment. The school was not prepared for external intervention and tended to be reactive when this inevitably occurred. When action had to be taken, discussions and decisions about externally imposed innovations tended to be protracted and often unfocussed, consuming large amounts of energy unproductively. As Pascale (1990) notes in his case study of General Motors, 'the very mechanisms that promote a strong culture easily turn inward and shut an organization off from external realities' (p. 259).

Third, and by contrast, the learning organization sees the environment differently. It does not look for clarity in the wrong places. It realizes that the outside world is and always will be messy, complex, and volatile. It picks and chooses its way, attempting to use certain events as catalysts for action, turn constraints into opportunities, and blunt or minimize other impositions that do not make sense. The key differences are that such organizations work at sense of purpose as a screening device (albeit continually unfinished), realize that the environment is not in the business of doing them any favors, and above all have an insatiable inquiry and learning orientation because they know that that is the only way to survive and prosper in complex environments.

Rosenholtz's 'moving' schools committed to continuous learning were not thrown by the latest state policies because these schools had a sense of what they were about, they were able to actively endorse and enlarge certain policies that provided opportunities for action, and blunt or openly challenge other policies that they perceived as wrong or undeveloped. The point is that they were 'in the game', able to hold their own in the give and take of policy deliberation.

Nias and her colleagues similarly found that the National Curriculum in England was reacted to differently by collaborative schools committed to teacher learning. They neither wholeheartedly rejected nor embraced the reform, but it did cause them to consider the whole school curriculum in a way that they would never have done without being open to the external stimulus. Nias *et al* (1992) conclude:

> the staff of these schools used an external initiative which they might have seen as a constraint to serve their own educational purposes. In the process they came to feel both that it was part of their own curricular thinking and that they were in control of it. That is, by the time that our fieldwork ended the staff in these schools felt that they 'owned' the relevant parts of the National Curriculum. (p. 195)

Learning organizations do not assume that they will always move forward. They know that events in the environment can thwart the most skilled group:

> Initiatives can be overtaken by events elsewhere (for example, legislation) or inhibited by changes in the school (for example, personnel). Either or both of these can have the effect of altering the pace and tempo of development. They can also make school initiatives redundant or adversely affect the staff to such an extent that developments temporarily halt or even regress. (*ibid*, p. 245)

Those individuals and organizations that are most effective do not experience fewer problems, less stressful situations, and greater fortune, *they just deal with them differently*. They literally cope with and even grow in the face of the same objective adversity that would destroy others with different mindsets and capacities (see Csikszentmihalyi, 1990).

In addition to a broadly-based orientation to the environment, specific partnerships and networks are essential. James Comer's School Development Program is a case in point because it so clearly marries moral purpose and change agentry in linking schools to their immediate environment over a period of time. The starting situation could hardly have been worse:

> The School Development Program (SDP) model was established in 1968 in two elementary schools as a collaborative effort between the Yale University Child Study Center and the New Haven School System. The two schools involved were the lowest achieving in the city, had poor attendance, and had

serious relationship problems among and between students, staff, and parents. Staff morale was low. Parents were angry and distrustful of the schools. Hopelessness and despair were pervasive. (Comer, 1992, p. 1)

The SDP model that developed over a period of years could not have been more faithful to what we know about effective change. The approach was to take a 'no fault' attitude to trying to understand and correct underlying problems. Says Comer, 'we eventually identified underlying problems on both sides — family stress and student under-development in areas needed for school success, as well as organiza-tional, management and child development knowledge and skills on the part of school staff' (p. 1).

The total program has nine components (three mechanisms, three operations, three guidelines). The mechanisms are: (i) a school planning management team representative of parents and school staff; (ii) a mental health team of social and psychological support staff; and (iii) a par-ents' program to increase the effectiveness and involvement of parents. The management team carries out three operations: (iv) a comprehensive school plan; (v) staff development; and (vi) periodic assessment and modification. The three guiding principles are: (vii) genuine collab-oration (you cannot paralyze the leader, and the leader cannot use the group as a 'rubber stamp'); (viii) consensual decision-making to avoid win-lose votes and failure to work at underlying issues; and (ix) a 'no-fault' problem solving approach.

The School Development Program has now spread to 200 schools and has a record of outstanding accomplishments given the problems that it has tackled. A variety of significant academic, behavioral, self-concept, and classroom and school climate effects have been documented in comparison with control group schools (Comer and Haynes, 1992).

On the one hand, the content of the nine-component model is impressive; it combines comprehensiveness, learning (staff development) for all — teachers, parents, children etc. — and sound processes. On the other hand, it is the respect for change and the conditions for long term progress that really stand out. Comer (1992) stresses:

It is not a 'quick fix', nor is it an 'add-on'. It is not just another new activity to be carved out along with all the other experi-ments being carved out in a school. It is a nine element process model . . . that takes significant time, commitment and energy to implement . . . and most importantly, the School Devel-opment Program produces desirable outcomes only after a cooperative and collaborative spirit exists throughout the school. (p. 9)

Most noteworthy, unlike most innovations that come quickly (and depart quickly), there was no fanfare in the early years. It took some fifteen years of developmental work in the two schools in New Haven before it spread to a small number of other schools. And it was not until 1991 and 1992 — almost twenty-five years later — that the first volume of SDP's newsletter appeared, and that any claim was made to have developed the know-how and technology to be able to provide training and support for others interested in implementing the program. Even then the advice is that interested partners have to be prepared to spend the time and energy over a period of years in order to develop their own clarity, and skills in collaborating in complex political environments before they will see results. The only failing of the SDP is that its pedagogical bases are not well described, and probably require further development (as compared for example, to Sizer's and Gardner's models).

The basic discovery arising from systemic thinking is that alliances are the bread and butter of learning organizations in dynamically complex societies. There are two reasons for this inevitable conclusion (and starting point for action). First, the problems are too difficult to solve by any one group; moreover, things that any agency does have consequences for all other relevant institutions so agencies affect each other in any case (usually negatively or arbitrarily). Second, in education a variety of stakeholders insist on having a voice in what is happening. The choice is whether such involvement will occur as mutually isolated influences working randomly or at cross purposes or will be developed through joint initiatives. Put directly, the complex difficulties of education for a learning society have no chance whatsoever of being addressed in the absence of alliances. Fiske (1992) summarizes the problem this way:

> Discussion of the relationship between public schools and their environment have all too often been muddied by two extreme positions. Some political and other leaders seem to view public schools as vehicles for single-handedly addressing every social malaise from racial injustice to the drug epidemic. Overwhelmed by the implication of such an assignment, educators respond by retreating to the opposite extreme. 'Just leave use alone', they say, 'so that we can do what we are supposed to do — teach children'. The first position is clearly unrealistic. No single

institution, least of all schools, is in a position to 'solve all of society's problems'. But the second position is a luxury educators can no longer afford. Schools may not be able to cure all social ills, but to succeed at all in their task of educating the next generation they must find ways of minimizing the negative impact of such problems on the teaching and learning process. To do this, they must find new allies and build new kinds of connections to the communities of which they are a part. (pp. 204–5)

Sarason (in press) puts it in different words:

If you enter the arena of educational reform with a 'find the villain' stance, you contribute to what is already a conceptual cloud chamber. There are no villains in the sense that this or that group in or related to the system deliberately made a bad situation worse . . . No major educational problem is only a 'within system' problem . . . That means that any action that stays within the system — based only on its own resources, personnel, decision-making processes and planning — is misconceived, parochial, and likely to fail. (pp. 33 and 35–6)

Incidentally, alliances, partnerships, consortia and collaboration all connote joint agreements and action over a period of time in which all parties learn to work differently and achieve qualitatively different results. Cooperation, communication, coordination all have their place, but do not go deeply enough. Schrage's (1990) definition of collaboration captures the idea nicely:

Collaboration is the process of *shared creation*: two or more individuals with complementary skills interacting to create a shared understanding that none had previously possessed or could have come to on their own. (p. 40)

Fortunately, there are more and more examples of virtually all types of agencies coming to the conclusion that alliances are essential — and they are backing it up with new policies, and action. We saw in the Comer program how schools, communities and a university have been collaborating for years to turn around one of the most debilitating and negative school situations to be found. Other school-university partnerships such as the Learning Consortium are described in chapter 6. Teacher unions in some instances have led the way in the

US in educational reform alliances (Shanker, 1990; and see Toch, 1991, chapter 5 for an analysis of the involvement of the American Federation of Teachers, and the National Education Association). In a remarkable document submitted to the Ontario government, the Ontario Teachers' Federation (OTF) (1992a) lays out a comprehensive statement on collaboration entitled *Beyond the Glitterspeak: Creating Genuine Collaboration in our Schools*. Stresses OTF, 'Education is shaped and owned by different stakeholders', and 'the days of regarding students, classrooms, or schools as isolated units are over' (pp. 4 and 5). The OTF document proceeds to map out the rationale and basis for action on several interrelated fronts:

- collaboration within the school (see also Fullan and Hargreaves, 1991);

- working with parents and community (the power of the evidence on parent-school partnerships 'is such that no reasonable case can be made for continued isolation' (p. 17));

- reaching out to the world of work ('the aims of business and a broad educational agenda are being drawn closer together' (p. 23));

- inter-ministerial and inter-school board collaboration (government agencies themselves must become collaborative internally, and externally).

Details of some of this new work of teacher unions are described in chapter 6.

The list of networking and alliances goes on. Along the same lines, business groups are forming agreements and consortia with educators, such as the National Alliance of Business (1989) in the US, the Conference Board of Canada (1991), and the Metropolitan Toronto Learning Partnership (1992) to name just a few. Moreover, philanthropic foundations are playing an increasingly prominent role not only as funders, but also as matchmakers and collaborative strategists (Evans, 1992; Ford, 1992; Wehlage, 1992). Nearly all of the major alliances and projects reported in this book have the active involvement of one or more foundations and businesses.

The eleven 'Winning Designs for a New Generation of American Schools' (*Education Week*, 1992, MecKlenburger, 1992) represents another formidable array of partnerships including one proposal, that has

Comer, Gardner, Sizer, Apple Computer Inc., and the National Alliance of Business on the team. In these projects we can predict that implementation problems will be massive, and that some very good ideas will be produced. But developing innovations is not a strategy in itself, if the ideas don't go anywhere. The Achilles heel of the New Generation of American Schools is the assumption that producing model schools will change the face of education. They can make a contribution, but local development *everywhere* is what is going to count.

In sum, 'no fault' partnerships among a variety of stakeholders in for the long haul, is another essential ingredient for learning individuals and learning organizations. But you have to know what you are doing (and why and how), because new levels of complexity are encountered. In any given collaborative effort, each partner will have to be willing to change its own culture, especially in terms of how it relates to other institutions. In our Learning Consortium, for example, we have drawn the following conclusions:

- Schools/school systems and universities (at least faculties of education) need each other to be successful.

- They are dissimilar in key aspects of structure, culture and reward systems.

- Working together potentially can provide the coherence, coordination, and persistence essential to teacher and school development.

- Both parties must work hard at working together — forging new structures, respecting each other's culture, and using shared experiences to problem-solve by incorporating the strengths of each culture.

- Strong partnerships will not happen by accident, good will or establishing *ad hoc* projects. They require new structures, new activities, and a rethinking of the internal workings of each institution as well as their inter-institutional workings. (Watson and Fullan, 1992, p. 219)

Even in working in particular collaboratives, learning organizations continually reach outside the partnerships in question. Successful collaborators 'use outsiders for complementary insights and information'; they solicit outside assistance, and 'are constantly on the lookout for people and information that will help them achieve their mission' (Schrage, 1990, pp. 160–1).

Learning to work with one or a few other agencies on a particular project, as difficult as it is, is the relatively easy part in entering the world of alliances. Given what we have said about dynamic complexity in the past three chapters, it is clear that learning organizations will have to be able to form and reform a *variety* of alliances simultaneously and over time. Particular collaboratives would end; others would start up. Only an active sense of moral purpose and the continual acquisition of the skills of change agentry will make it possible to be an effective partner, and to navigate this territory, staying on course even when the rest of the environment doesn't seem to be cooperating.

Recall Land and Jarman's (1992) definition of growth: '(the capacity to continuously make) more extensive and increasingly complex connections inside the growing organism and with the varied outside environments' (p. 30). This will not be easy work because many of the partnerships that we are talking about involve individuals and groups coming to the table with different experiences, viewpoints, world views and imagined solutions. But this is the very point — it is these differences that contain the necessary ingredients for productive action. In the same way that 'problems are our friends' (chapter 3), differences across stakeholders are also our friends because negotiating these differences into a new shared reality is where new solutions lie. Thus, 'the growth potential of any system is fulfilled by connecting with the different and dissimilar rather than building on similarities' (Land and Jarman, 1992, p. 27).

We have one other aspect of the environment to consider, one that is both of practical significance and of metaphysical dimensions — *ultimately we are all 'out there'.*

We Are All Out There

In a direct way we are all out there because organizations are not stable. Even if we stay in the same organization for long periods of time, others will come and go, changing the organization. And most of us will join a number of organizations over our careers. We have a vested interest in what goes on in the environment. We need to take responsibility beyond our own immediate situation, if for no other reason than self-interest.

To take a small scale example, imagine the principal who aggressively recruits the best collaborative teachers from other schools while transferring the least effective to whomever will take them. This is ultimately self-defeating. First, what goes around, comes around! Eventually, you too will have to take your turn in receiving teachers discarded by other schools. Therefore, aggressive selection will only yield temporary success. Second, while such selection may create collaborative schools, it will not create collaborative systems. Schools that select aggressively and have unusual powers to hire and fire become innovative exceptions. Infuriatingly, they are then often held up by their systems as beacons of improvement which the rest, creamed of their best teachers, are expected to, but are frustratingly unable to follow.

Individually and together, principals have a responsibility to help upgrade the learning opportunities for all teachers in the system. Acting in narrowly competitive ways, prematurely giving up on some of one's own staff, and investing too much in the selection of the fittest, produce short term advantages at best — and even then, only for a minority of schools, not for systems as a whole (see Fullan and Hargreaves, 1991, pp. 96–7).

But there is another, fundamental way in which we are all out there, and it is the essence of dynamic complexity, and systems thinking. Land and Jarman (1992) state it as 'Everything exists as sets of connections with the world around it' (p. 103). They stress that the notion that things are separate is factually wrong. Rather:

> Everything and everybody is connected. Everything affects everything else. No matter how different, no matter how far away, we are all part of an interconnected whole . . . the fact is that no real division can be found between ourselves, other people, and the world around us — *unless we create it in our minds.* (p. 104)

Csikszentmihalyi (1990) calls it personal and 'universal flow'. Senge (1990) refers to it as 'the indivisible whole', the realization that the earth is both small and of utmost significance to us:

> The earth is an indivisible whole, just as each of us is an indivisible whole. Nature (and that includes us) is not made up of parts within wholes. It is made up of wholes within wholes. All boundaries, national boundaries included, are fundamentally arbitrary. We invent them and then, ironically, we find ourselves trapped within them. (p. 371)

Senge (1990) quotes Einstein:

> . . . (the human being) experiences himself, his thoughts and feelings as something separated from the rest — a kind of optical delusion of our consciousness. This delusion is a kind of prison for us, restricting us to our personal desires and to affection for a few persons nearest to us. Our task must be to free ourselves from this prison by widening our circle of compassion to embrace all living creatures and the whole of nature in its beauty. (p. 170)

Moral purpose writ large! But it is the case that being 'committed to the whole' is of essential practical value to surviving productively in complex global societies, and is a necessary component of meaningful existence. Productive alliances, in other words, know no boundaries, because change forces know no boundaries.

A View from Above

People, especially those in line authority, often want other parts of the organization to become learning entities pursuing continuous improvements. District staff expect schools to act that way, governments want local districts and communities to be like that. If one is part of a central group, how can one promote learning in local jurisdictions? It is not easy, but some guidelines point the way.

First, ask yourself if your own department or central organization is a learning one, i.e., does it practice what it preaches? If the answer is no, then you cannot expect local groups to take you seriously. Role models and associated actions matter a great deal. The starting point is to get one's own house in order (although individuals can take effective action despite the organizations they are in — see chapter 7). Pascale (1990) calls this the 'real revolution' in the Ford Motor Company's successful transformation, 'the sincerity and persistence of [senior executives] that *they* needed to change if Ford was going to change. This is the rarest, yet most essential, ingredient in successful change: top executives who are willing to suffer and change themselves' (p. 138).

Second, you can't mandate what matters (chapter 3). Multi-unit learning organizations evolve in constant tension between the center and the local setting. Simultaneous top-down/bottom-up strategies must co-exist and reinforce each other. According to Pascale, organizations to be successful must continually manage the constructive tension of 'fit' and 'split' operations — sometimes integrating, at other times decentralizing, and often doing both at the same time with respect to different functions.

Several examples of how this operates now exist in the business and educational literature. Assuming that we recognize that effective change and learning always occurs locally, the legitimate worry of central decision-makers is 'how can locally controlled organizations achieve coordination, synergy between business units, and collaborative efforts toward common corporate-wide objectives' (Senge, 1990, p. 288). Senge responds:

> It is no coincidence that the (leading organizations) such as Royal Dutch/Shell and Hanover Insurance, have a high degree of local control . . . While traditional organizations require management systems that control people's behavior, learning organizations invest in improving the quality of thinking, the capacity for reflection and team learning, and the ability to develop shared visions and shared understandings of complex business issues. It is these capabilities that will allow learning organizations to be both more locally controlled *and* more well coordinated than their hierarchical predecessors. (p. 289)

Sarason (1990) draws a similar conclusion about schools:

> How do you build in self-correcting forums and mechanisms so absent in our schools? Put that way, the task is not evaluation in the narrow sense but development of an organizational culture that makes self-correction a norm and not a war. (p. 129)

The reason that I dwell on local learning is not ideological preference, but the fact that it is the only conclusion one can arrive at after understanding the dynamics of change. Any assumption that control can be managed at the top of complex organizations is an illusion (Senge, 1990). Thus, the new role of central management, as Stacey (1992) stresses, is practising and creating the conditions for organizational members to develop the core capacities for contending with the forces of change:

> When the future is unknowable, managers cannot install techniques, procedures, structures, and ideologies to control long-term outcomes . . . It is through political interaction and

complex learning that businesses create and manage their unknowable futures. (pp. 202–203)

Hampden-Turner's (1992) review of the Hanover Insurance Company provides a good illustration of the key issues. Investment in continuous skill development at all levels operates in a *negotiated* system of local and central give and take. The dilemma, successfully managed by Hanover was:

> how to make local branch staff stronger and more self-reliant, while also making the staff at the national office strong, capable, and responsive. There were two perils to be avoided: A strong central staff that suppressed local initiatives and made branches dependent, and a strong local staff that resented any interference from national HQ as an infringement of their autonomy. (p. 25)

Hampden-Turner found that Hanover constantly works on the attainment of a larger vision which is tested by specific information and numbers gathered by the organization. It is recognized that local units are comparable in some respects, and different in others. Thus, the center and the locals negotiate goals, develop strategies for success and seek data in relation to agreed upon directions. Seely Brown (1991) of Xerox says that one of the main jobs of central management is to encourage and sponsor local partnerships (again connecting to the environment), and then to 'harvest local innovations' (p. 106).

The same conclusions hold for school-center relationships. In the Learning Consortium we call it managing school-district co-development (Fullan, in press). The four school districts (averaging 60,000 students and 125 schools each) are constantly engaged in strategies to manage and negotiate the tensions that come with simultaneous school and system development. Some of the main components of this attempt at correlated development include: the establishment and continuing refinement of a broad-based mission statement and strategic plan; the development and support of school plans; performance appraisal linked to staff development; selection and promotion processes geared to change effectiveness; a systematic commitment to professional development (both school-based and system-related); devolution of resources to the school-community level; and a district coordinated assessment procedure.

The notion of schools as learning organizations leads to new approaches to control and accountability. Traditional approaches to assessment fail because they are detached from effective means of acting on the data. As Darling-Hammond and Ascher (1992) say, 'performance indicators . . . are information for the accountability system; they are not the system itself. Accountability (i.e., responsible practice and responsiveness to clients) occurs only when a useful set of processes exists for interpreting and acting on the information' (p. 2). And, as we have seen earlier, different measures of student learning will be needed. Moreover, learning organizations are more holistically accountable as they work more systemically. In the words of Darling-Hammond and Ascher:

> Assessment data are helpful to the extent that they provide relevant, valid, timely, and useful information about how much individual students are learning and how well schools are serving them. But these kinds of data are only a tiny part of the total accountability process. Accountability also encompasses how a school or school system hires, evaluates, and supports its staff; how it relates to students and parents; how it manages its daily affairs; how it makes decisions; how it ensures that the best available knowledge will be acquired and used; how it evaluates its own functioning, as well as students' progress; how it tackles problems; and how it provides incentives for continual improvement. (p. 2; see also Hill and Bonan, 1991)

Whether locally or centrally, the ultimate conclusion for the learning organization in dynamically complex environments, is that change forces come at us in surprising and unplanned ways. Thus, the capacity 'to live in a state of continuous imbalance' is essential (Pascale, 1990, p. 174). I have argued that organizations that work on the core capacities of change agentry — personal vision, mastery, inquiry and collaboration — will fare better under these circumstances. The key features of this new organization are summarized by Pascale — one that:

(i) entails a holistic rather than piecemeal view of organizations;
(ii) embraces contentions as a source of energy and renewal, and
(iii) builds a climate that encourages people to identify with company goals and apply their full energies to achieving them.

The net effect of these factors must be pronounced enough to prod an organization into a constant state of restlessness, yet not so rending that it becomes destructive. (p. 174)

Most organizations that have attempted such a transformation, experience great difficulties in the early stages. The factor that distinguishes those that move ahead is whether they *learn* from their experiences. To be able to do this depends very much on the learning orientations and capacities of the organization's members. The capacity to learn on a continuous basis is not just for formal leaders, but for all members. Thus, the skills and habits of everyday teachers are central to the future of learning societies. For schools, nothing can rival teacher education as a source of unfullfilled promises for increasing the learning capacity of its organizational members.

Chapter 6

Teacher Education: Society's Missed Opportunity

Society has failed its teachers in two senses of the word. It gives teachers failing grades for not producing better results. At the same time, it does not help improve the conditions that would make success possible. A real catch 22. I shall also make it clear in this chapter that teacher educators, and teachers have failed themselves in not taking action to help break the catch 22 cycle. Systems don't change when people wait for somone else to correct the problem (chapter 7).

Despite the rhetoric about teacher education in today's society, there does not seem to be a real belief or confidence that investing in teacher education will yield results. Perhaps deep down many leaders believe that teaching is not all that difficult. After all, most leaders have spent thousands of hours in the classroom and are at least armchair experts. And they know that scores of unqualified teachers are placed in classrooms every year and required to learn on the job. In addition, investing in teacher education is not a short-term strategy. With all the problems facing us demanding immediate solution it is easy to overlook a preventative strategy that would take several years to have an impact. When a crisis occurs you have to deal with it. A course of action that is aimed at preventing a crisis, despite being much less expensive in the mid to long term, is much harder to come by.

Yet, it should be clear, if you have read the previous chapters, that a high quality teaching force — always learning — is the *sine qua non* of coping with dynamic complexity, i.e., of helping to produce citizens who can manage their lives and relate to those around them in a continually changing world. There are no substitutes to having better teachers.

The teaching profession is in better shape than the medical profession was in 1910 when Abraham Flexner condemned the poor quality of preparation of doctors and called for a wholesale upgrading. But this is not saying much — eighty years is a long time to be behind. However, the real problem is that there is not the sense of practical urgency and clarity of action in the 1990s to do something about teacher education. Teacher education still has the honour of being simultaneously the worst problem and the best solution in education. We need desperately to size up the problem, and see what can be done to make the career-long continuum of teacher learning a reality.

Sizing Up the Problem

Remember Rachel B (chapter 4). She came into teaching highly motivated to make a contribution. Despite all kinds of attempts to become a good teacher, by the end of her second year she began to withdraw from her work, putting in minimal effort, wondering what to do about her future but not taking any steps to change it. She has another thirty-five years of routine cynical work before her. How many students, and how many colleagues will she unwittingly affect adversely?

It is fairly easy to size-up the nature and scope of the problem. I shall be mercifully brief about it. The problem begins with teacher preparation programs. Howey and Zimpher's (1989) detailed case studies of six universities in the US enabled them to generate fourteen attributes that would be necessary for program coherence, which they find lacking in existing programs, factors such as: programs based on clear conceptions of teaching and schooling; programs that have clear thematic qualities; faculty coalescing around experimental or alternative programs that have distinctive qualities; working with student cohort groups; adequate curriculum materials and a well-conceived laboratory component; articulation between on campus programming and field-based student teaching; direct linkage to research and development knowledge bases; and regular program evaluation.

Goodlad (1990a) and his associates in a comprehensive investigation of twenty-nine universities are even more damning. Among their main findings:

1 The preparation programs in our sample made relatively little use of the peer socialization processes employed in some other fields of professional preparation. There were few efforts to organize incoming candidates into cohort groups or to do so at some later stage. Consequently, students' interactions about their experiences were confined for the most part to formal classes (where the teaching is

heavily didactic). The social, intellectual, and professional isolation of teachers, so well described by Dan Lortie, begins in teacher education. This relatively isolated individualism in preparation seems ill-suited to developing the collegiality that will be demanded later in site-based school renewal.

2   The rapid expansion of higher education, together with unprecedented changes in academic life, have left professors confused over the mission of higher education and uncertain of their role in it. Although the effects of these changes in academic life transcend schools and departments, the decline of teaching in favor of research in most institutions of higher education has helped lower the status of teacher education. In regional public universities, once normal schools and teachers colleges, the situation has become so bad that covering up their historic focus on teacher education is virtually an institutional rite of passage. Teaching in the schools and teacher education seem unable to shake their condition of status deprivation.

3   There are serious disjunctures in teacher education programs: between the arts and sciences portion and that conducted in the school or department of education, from component to component of the so-called professional sequence, and between the campus-based portion and the school-based portion . . . It is also clear from our data that the preparation under way in the programs we studied focussed on *classrooms* but scarcely at all on *schools*.

4   Courses in the history, philosophy, and social foundations of education . . . have seriously eroded. (pp. 700–1)

The beginning years of teaching do not fare any better. Induction programs to support beginning teachers are still very much in the minority, and good ones are rare, despite our very clear knowledge of the needs of beginning teachers, and despite the high probability that solid induction programs represent one of the most cost-efficient preventative strategies around. We have known about these problems for a couple of decades (but not about the details of their solution, which I take up in the next section). McDonald and Elias' (1980) four-volume study still represents the norm. They summarize their findings:

1 Almost all teachers experience the transition period into teaching as the most difficult aspect of their teaching life and career. There apparently are some teachers who move into teaching smoothly and efficiently, but the majority report the period as one of great difficulty and even trauma.

2 The major kinds of problems and difficulties that teachers experience are readily identifiable. Most of them relate to the management and conduct of instruction. These problems are so critical that it is easy to overlook the equally obvious fact that the range of problems includes difficulties with evaluating pupils, being evaluated by the administration, working with parents, developing a consistent teaching style, finding out how the school functions, knowing the rules that must be followed, and a variety of other problems.

3 The least studied aspect of this transition period is the fear, anxiety, and feelings of isolation and loneliness that appear to characterize it. There is sufficient information in existing reports to indicate that these feelings are not uncommon; however, individual conversations with teachers are far more revealing than the current literature.

4 Almost all teachers report that they went through this transition period 'on their own'. They had little or no help available, and found help only through their own initiative. This help usually took the form of seeking out some other teacher in whom they could confide . . .

5 There is probably a strong relationship between how teachers pass through the transition period and how likely they are to progress professionally to high levels of competence and endeavor. (Vol. I, pp. 42–3)

The rest of the career isn't any more encouraging (see Fullan, 1991, chapter 15). From a learning point of view, the working conditions in most schools are not such that teachers become better by virtue of being on the staff of learning organizations. If they do become better it is likely despite the systems in which they find themselves. And, we haven't even introduced the problem of working in difficult urban multicultural schools. The American Research Institute (1992) rank ordered the ten most stressful occupations. Number one was 'inner city teacher' — ahead of policemen, and air traffic controllers.

One can find pockets of success, and we will move shortly to see what it would take to extend these efforts. Nonetheless, I believe that the above describes the modal state of teacher education across the career. Teachers are finding it more and more difficult to believe that they are in a noble profession, working diligently and skillfully for the betterment of their clients. Compared to the past it is easier to feel burnt-out, harder to feel appreciated and satisfied, and it is more likely that good and knowledgeable people will not be attracted to or want to stay in the profession.

What To Do

The problem in other words is enormous. We don't have a learning profession. Teachers and teacher educators do not know enough about subject matter, they don't know enough about how to teach, and they don't know enough about how to understand and influence the conditions around them. Above all, teacher education — from initial preparation to the end of the career — is not geared towards continuous learning.

Making explicit and strengthening moral purpose and change agentry and their connection is the key to altering the profession. When one examines the history of teacher education it is surprising to find that the idea of teachers as moral change agents has been around a long time. I want to start then, by considering why these earlier versions have not caught on, as a point of departure for what needs to be done.

Initial Teacher Preparation

The federally sponsored Teacher Corps and Trainers of Teacher Trainers (TTT) programs in the US merit close consideration. They occurred a quarter of a century ago, focussed on societal improvement and promptly disappeared without a trace. What can we learn from these efforts?

Between 1965 and 1975 the Teacher Corps prepared 11,000 teachers. The program 'tested on a national scale the hypothesis that an internship model of teacher preparation could serve as a mechanism for improving education for the disadvantaged' (Weiner, 1992, p. 9; see also Drummond and Andrews, 1980). The program explicitly set out to produce an influx of 'change agents' (using that very phrase). Groups of interns enrolled for a two-year on-the-job training program while gradually increasing their teaching responsibility under a 'master teacher'. At local sites, school districts and universities were to cooperate in delivering the program. Aside from its quantitative expansion over a decade, the program never had its desired impact. Defined as change agents, interns and project personnel clashed with regular school staff and were frequently rejected.

The TTT program began in 1967 and by 1970 was operating on fifty-seven sites. Again the goal was social change — the improvement of education for the disadvantaged — this time by focussing on teacher educators who could in turn improve the quality of teacher preparation programs and their graduates. One of its central tenets was the concept of 'parity', which 'was defined as the participation of schools of education, liberal arts colleges, public schools and communities in planning and conducting teacher education programs' (Weiner, 1992, p. 9).

The life-span of TTT was a short six years (1967–73). During this time a range of programs were developed which were so wide in content and structure that they 'resist summary'. Various projects attempted curriculum reform and field-based training in schools. Projects were plagued with problems. One project director resigned shortly after the program began stating that the guidelines 'to identify groups of change agents among the professors of teacher education, professors of liberal arts, public school teachers, parents, community representatives, and college students' were too vague. It was never clear in the TTT initiative how teacher educators themselves were to improve other than by receiving funds and a general mandate to reform teacher education.

Both Teacher Corps and TTT were certainly victims of what I earlier called large-scale tinkering — 'a clumsy attempt to mend something'. The main reasons for their failure in my view were:

1 The programs were based on extremely vague conceptions. Having an ideology is not the same as having conceptions and ideas of what should be done and how it should be done.

2 They focussed on individuals without taking into account institutions.

3 They were non-systemic, i.e., they gave little thought to changes in interinstitutional relationships (for example, between schools and universities).

4   They ignored the knowledge and skill base that would be required. (ideology and opportunity were to be sufficient)

5   To the extent that they worked on change — albeit clumsily — most of the effort was directed at school systems, not at universities. Even the TTT program which had the latter focus shifted most of its attention to the school milieu.

We have a modern version of teacher education as social change agentry which has been well worked out by Liston and Zeichner (1991). These authors call for a 'social reconstructionist' agenda for teacher education. Liston and Zeichner advocate that teacher educators should be:

(1) directly involved in a teacher education program in some capacity (e.g., as a teacher or administrator); (2) engaged in political work within colleges and universities; (3) actively supportive of efforts within the public schools to create more democratic work and learning environments; (4) engaged in political work within professional associations and in relation to state educational agencies; (5) working for democratic changes aimed at achieving greater social justice in other societal and political areas. (p. 188)

In commenting on current reform proposals in teacher education — such as the Carnegie Report (1986) and the Holmes Group (1986 and 1990) — Liston and Zeichner state: 'we strongly object to the almost complete absence in some of the reports of proposals to enhance the moral consciousness, social and political commitment, and capability of teachers to work toward the elimination of social, educational, economic, and political inequalities' (pp. 217–8). To their credit both authors are directly involved (in two different universities) in developing and implementing such programs.

Despite some valuable ideas and components I don't think the Liston and Zeichner proposal will fly. They have on the one hand, addressed the 'vague conception' problem. Their proposal is clear, and they have implemented aspects of it in their own institutions. On the other hand, the fatal flaw is that taking on society is too ambitious. We cannot expect the vast majority of teachers and teacher educators to engage in political work, establish better democracies and reduce social injustices, even in their own baliwicks. Stated at this level, it is too daunting, too ambitious. Some teachers may very well spend their time in this arena, and all the better. But for the majority of teachers they must find their moral niche closer to the individual student. If these teachers can also see the causal relationship between working conditions at the school level and their ability to be effective in the classroom they will be motivated to work with others on school and school system change. I believe that reform in teacher education must focus on developing and bringing together two broad themes:

1   It must reestablish the moral purpose of teaching (defined as making a difference in the lives of more and more individual students).

2   It must establish and continue to develop the knowledge and skill-base required to accomplish (1) including knowledge and skills required to change organizations and to contend with the forces of change in complex environments.

We should then expect all teachers to pursue actively and explicitly moral purpose and local improvement of conditions needed to support continuous change. We have seen that moral purpose in teaching and teacher education has been around a long time, but it has never become established. It is time to reintroduce moral purpose explicitly into the institutional objectives of teacher education and teaching (see chapter 2; and Goodlad, 1990b; Sirotnik, 1990). It can be made meaningful at the individual level because it is close to the hearts of good teacher candidates and teachers already. Moral purpose in the classroom can be further elevated as teachers realize that making a difference in the lives of one or more students makes a contribution to the improvement of society in both social and economic terms. Moral purpose needs to be highlighted and reconceptualized as a change theme.

It is one thing to be noble, it is another thing to know what you are doing. Another missing element — and we have further to go on this one — concerns the establishment and continuous development of the knowledge and skill base that will be required to (a) teach effectively a variety of individuals; and (b) influence the school and other working conditions that affect how well we will be able to do (a). Teachers cannot have an impact in the classroom unless they also have an impact on altering the working conditions that surround the classroom.

The absence of a strong publicly stated knowledge base allows the misconception to continue that any smart person can teach. After visiting fourteen colleges of education across the US, Kramer (1992) concludes:

> Everything [a person] needs to know about how to teach could
> be learned by intelligent people in a single summer of well-
> planned instruction. (p. 214)

In a twisted way there is some truth to this observation. It is true
in the sense that many people did and still do take such minimal instruction, and manage to have a career in teaching. It is true also that
some people with a strong summer program would end up knowing
as much or more as others who take a weak year long program. In her
journey, Kramer found plenty of examples of moral purpose — caring
people, committed to social equality: 'Everywhere, I found idealistic
people eager to do good' (p. 209). What she found wanting was an
emphasis on knowledge and understanding. Caring and competence
are, of course, not mutually exclusive (indeed this is the point), but
they can seem that way when the knowledge base is so poorly
formulated.

I will not spend much time on the important area of recruitment
and selection into the profession (for the best discussion see Schlechty,
1990, chapter 1). In many ways an 'if you build it they will come'
strategy is called for. It is self-defeating to seek candidates who turn
out to be better than the programs they enter. What is needed is a
combination of selection criteria that focus on academics as well as
experience (related for example, to moral purpose), sponsorship for
underrepresented groups, and a damn good program. Schlechty adds
this valuable perspective:

> Teacher education could, I believe, be much improved if those
> who sought entry could be brought to understand that learning
> to teach requires considerable investment of time and talent.
> Thus, it is in the interest of quality teacher education to create
> conditions in which talented individuals are willing to enter
> programs that require them to undergo a longer period of
> development than is commonly the case in present teacher
> education programs. (p. 22)

To do this, stronger programs are required.

In short, a key obstacle in the evolution of teaching as a profession
is an inadequately defined knowledge base about teaching and teacher
education. Lichtenstein, McLaughlin and Knudsen (1992) identify this
problem in their examination of restructuring. They argue that the
expansion of teachers roles and responsibilities will never succeed
unless there is a corresponding expansion of teacher knowledge.

'Knowledge', they say 'is an elemental, irreducible aspect of teacher empowerment' (p. 40). Lichtenstein *et al* elaborate:

> The knowledge that empowers teachers to pursue their craft with confidence, enthusiasm, and authority is knowledge of the teaching profession, in the broadest possible sense.

> We distilled the essential kinds of knowledge empowered teachers possessed into three overlapping areas:

> • knowledge of professional community
> • knowledge of education policy
> • knowledge of subject area (p. 41)

Competence breeds confidence. In this respect, Sarason (in press) documents how far we have to go in teacher education in our own eyes as well as those of society. Sarason takes as his point of departure the thesis that attempting to *repair* schools (while this should continue) is far less effective than trying to *prevent* problems from accumulating. He calls for better preparatory programs for educators — teachers and administrators alike — that could serve the goal of producing more effective educators and change agents.

Sarason devotes an entire chapter to the 1910 Flexner Report on *Medical Education in the United States and Canada*. Flexner's solution was to outline a preparatory medical program that integrated hands-on laboratory work and clinical experience with supervised interactions in hospitals. As Sarason observes, 'it never entered Flexner's thinking to come up with recommendations for improving the practice of *existing* physicians' (p. 114). Lest I be misinterpreted let me make two additional points. Medical education has its share of problems and is no panacea, but it is the case that the preparation of doctors (and air traffic controllers etc.) is taken much more seriously than the preparation of teachers. Second, my emphasis on preparation is not to deny the importance of in-service education, but rather to highlight the fact that teacher preparation is so sorely neglected.

Teacher educators like other would-be change agents must take some initiative themselves, which is now happening on several fronts. At the University of Toronto we embarked on a major reform effort in 1988. With a faculty of some ninety staff and 1100 full time students in one-year post baccalaureate teacher certification program, we began by piloting a number of field-based options in partnerships with school systems (see Faculty of Education, University of Toronto, 1992a). At the same time a large number of new staff were recruited, many of whom work in teams with veteran faculty members. Consistent with lesson 4 ('Visions and Strategic Planning Come Later', chapter 3) we are now attempting to consolidate our initial experiences with reform into a more coherent vision and more systematic redesign of the program. In 1991, I prepared a short paper for our Strategic Planning Committee. I took as a starting point the following premise: *Faculties of education should not be advocating things for teachers or schools that they are not capable of practising themselves.* I used a hypothetical 'best faculty of education in the country' metaphor as a vehicle for formulating ten key characteristics. Specifically I suggested that such a faculty would:

1   Commit itself to producing teachers who are agents of educational and social improvement.

2   Commit itself to continuous improvement through program innovation and evaluation.

3   Value and practise exemplary teaching.

4   Engage in constant inquiry.

5   Model and develop life-long learning among staff and students.

6   Model and develop collaboration among staff and students.

7   Be respected and engaged as a vital part of the university as a whole.

8   Form partnerships with schools and other agencies.

9   Be visible and valued internationally in a way that contributes locally and globally.

10   Work collaboratively to build regional, national, and international networks.

To illustrate, consider items three and six. Item three: it would seem self-evident that faculties of education would stand for exemplary teaching among their own staff. Faculties of education have some excellent (and poor) teachers, but I would venture to say that hardly any have effective *institutional* mechanisms for working on the improvement of their own teaching. Item six: many faculties of education advocate collegiality and collaborative work cultures for schools, and some participate in 'professional development schools'. This leads to two embarrassing questions. First, to what extent are teacher preparation programs designed so that student teachers deliberately practice, get better at, and develop the habits and skills of collaboration? Even more embarrassing: to what extent do university professors (arts and science as well as education) value and practice collaboration in their own teaching and scholarship?

With such guiding principles and some experience with them in practice through our pilot projects, at the University of Toronto we have recently proceeded to the matter of redesigning the entire program. The Restructuring Committee has proposed the following six images for teacher preparation:

Key Images for Teacher Preparation

We believe that the role played by teachers is vital to the future of society. Initial teacher preparation must provide prospective teachers with the knowledge, skills and attitudes that will form a strong foundation for effective teaching, and for continuous learning and development throughout their careers. Teachers can make learning exciting and productive for students if their own learning is exciting and productive. Every teacher should become an agent of school and social improvement pursued through the following six goals. Every teacher should be knowledgeable about, committed to and skilled in:

1   Working with *all* students in an equitable, effective and caring manner by respecting diversity in relation to ethnicity, race, gender, and special needs of each learner.

2   Being active learners who continuously seek, assess, apply and communicate knowledge as reflective practitioners throughout their careers.

3   Developing and applying knowledge of curriculum, instruction, principles of learning, and evaluation needed to implement and monitor effective and evolving programs for all learners.

4   Initiating, valuing and practising collaboration and partnerships with students, colleagues, parents, community, government, and social and business agencies.

5   Appreciating and practising the principles, ethics and legal responsibilities of teaching as a profession.

6   Developing a personal philosophy of teaching which is informed by and contributes to the organizational, community, societal and global contexts of education. (Faculty of Education, University of Toronto, 1992b)

We are now working on the task of developing the actual program, curriculum and teaching designs. Everything we know about the complexities of change applies in spades to the reform of higher education intitutions. Nonetheless, after four years we have made good progress and look forward to the next four years as the telling ones i.e., the years when more comprehensive and systematic reform will be put into place.

Similar developments are happening elsewhere. *The Network of Fifteen* project (Howey, 1992) which is now being proposed, is a case in point. Fifteen universities in the US and Canada, are involved. I reproduce the abstract of the proposal in full because it is such an unusual reform effort:

This proposal addresses a matter of grave concern: preparing high quality teachers for urban schools. Recent data indicate that the great majority of graduating teachers neither believe that they are prepared to teach in these schools, where the needs are the greatest, nor are they disposed to do so.

In order to address this problem a network of fifteen respected institutions who prepare teachers in major urban areas in the United States and Canada have committed themselves to a major restructuring of their teacher education programs. The departure point for the project is to look inward, and with the help of outstanding teachers, engage in a sustained or comprehensive program of faculty development to drive this restructuring. The conception of teacher preparation embraced by the network intersects in a major way with urban elementary and secondary partnership schools and with parallel school restructuring efforts at those sites. The two must proceed hand in hand.

The primary change strategy for this major undertaking is anchored in the preparation and continuing support of leadership teams in each school and college. While this is a concept that has proven successful in some school reform efforts, it is a concept foreign to this point in time in higher education. The dean or director of teacher education will work with three other faculty or administrative leaders in an interrelated four-pronged leadership development activity focused on:

(i) organizational functioning and professional culture;
(ii) faculty development and especially the improvement of teaching;
(iii) major alterations in pre-service programs preparing teachers for urban settings; and
(iv) the development of a clinical faculty.

These leadership teams will engage in regular cycles of training and then collectively serve as the catalyst for major restructuring at their home site. They will also involve their colleagues in elementary and secondary schools in major ways in these restructuring efforts.

A second distinctive feature of the project, beyond the unique, differentiated leadership focus, is the concept of *network* which has been negotiated by the institutions involved. Eight goals which a network can enable, better than individual institutions, are identified, including political action to influence needed policy changes. Also, the Ohio State University serving as the hub of the network will facilitate various types of exchanges enabled by participation in the network across the fifteen institutions.

Among the outcomes envisioned over the three year project are: the development of high quality leadership training activities and materials which can be employed in other institutions, case studies of each change effort, the implementation of distinctive urban teacher education programs, assessments of a variety of faculty development efforts, and the design of instructional materials and artifacts which can be employed in preservice programs preparing teachers for urban settings. (Howey, 1992)

We at the University of Toronto are one of the fifteen because the network so clearly builds on what we are attempting. We see it as a major vehicle for developing a better knowledge base in terms of program design, curriculum, and instruction for teacher education, and for continuing to make the structural and normative changes necessary to support programmatic reform.

The Holmes Group has also turned its attention to colleges of education in its forthcoming *Tomorrow's Colleges of Education*, the third in a series following *Tomorrow's Teachers* (1986), and *Tomorrow's Schools* (1990). The report is not yet available, but it should put the spotlight on colleges and universities. An important question is how much of a focus will there be on the difficulties and needed strategies for the *internal* development of faculties of education, as well as their relationships with the rest of the university, and with schools.

The new National Board for Professional Teaching Standards (1992) in the US while not directly related to teacher preparation should also contribute to the formulation of a knowledge base as it pursues its central policy statement, 'What Teachers Should Know and Be Able to Do'. The NBPTS is well on its way to raising the $50 million budget it has targeted. It describes its basic purpose:

> The National Board for Professional Teaching Standards is a non-profit, non-governmental organization. Our purpose is to improve student learning in America's schools by developing a system of advanced, voluntary certification for elementary and secondary school teachers. The National Board will establish high and rigorous standards for what teachers should know and be able to do, and certify teachers who meet those standards. In addition, we are addressing education policy and reform issues such as teacher preparation, teacher recruitment (especially among minorities), and the quality of the school as a workplace for students and teachers. (p. 2)

Development work is underway in establishing standards (for what teachers should know and be able to do) in early childhood, English language arts, art, music, science, mathematics, social studies, guidance counselling and in a number of other areas. As before, educators are cautioned to be critical consumers. We know about the uncertainties of teaching and teaching as a craft. But in the same way that useful progress is being made on better ways of displaying student learning, it can also be made with teacher learning. Teacher standards and portfolios can become effective strategies for teacher learning (see Lichtenstein, Rubin and Grant, 1992). However, standards, no matter how sophisticated and enlightened, are not in themselves strategies for improvement. Darling-Hammond and Ascher's (1992) comment on accountability systems for schools is equally applicable to teacher knowledge, namely that 'performance indicators' by themselves do not constitute an accountability system. The latter occurs 'only when a useful set of processes exists for interpreting and acting on the information' (p. 2).

To those who eschew the pursuit of a more defined knowledge base for teacher preparation, let us remember that teacher education is notorious for having vague conceptions, lack of program coherence, and weak or non-existent measures of outcomes. This is why they are so vulnerable. This is why for example, we see proposals such as the recent one in England and Wales in which 80 per cent of initial teacher preparation was to be in schools, and 20 per cent in universities with resources to be reallocated accordingly (Department of Education and Science, 1992). It has since been reduced to a 67:33 per cent ratio partly in realization of what it would take to increase the school's capacity to play this new role. Partnerships are essential, as I have argued, but this particular proposal pays almost no attention to the development of the knowledge-base that would be required, vastly underestimates the problems of identifying, preparing and supporting skilled mentors, and is silent on the difficulties of establishing collaborative relationships between universities and school systems.

To summarize: it is necessary for faculties of education to redesign their programs to focus directly on developing the beginner's knowledge base for effective teaching *and* the knowledge base for making changes in the conditions that affect teaching. Sarason (in press) puts it this way: 'Is it asking too much of preparatory programs to prepare their students for a "real world" which they must understand *and seek to change* if as persons and professionals they are to grow, not only to survive' (p. 252, my emphasis). Goodlad (1991) asks a similar question: 'Are a large percentage of these educators thoroughly grounded in the knowledge and skills required to bring about meaningful change?' (p. 4)

Reforming teacher preparation institutions, like any attempt to change complex traditional organizations, faces enormous obstacles. But even universities change under certain conditions. Sarason names four conditions. When:

- recognition by the public and socially-politically influential groups that a set of interrelated problems is adversely affecting societal stability or health or values;

- a similar recognition by significant individuals and groups within the university;
- the willingness of public and private agencies to help fund the change;
- the perceived leadership of prestigious universities who appear to be accepting of the change. (p. 144)

Not the least of these conditions is the necessity of teacher educators to take the initiative. It is a central theme of this book that systems don't change themselves. Again Sarason captures it: 'as long as educators see themselves as lacking the power to change anything in a meaningful way — waiting for Godot for salvation from others somewhere in an uncomprehending world — they will remain part of the problem' (p. 217). The development of a knowledge base for change is a powerful potential asset for altering the quality and the status of teacher preparation. Ironically, nothing should come more naturally to higher education institutions — since they are in the learning business — than to lead the way in helping to develop teaching as a learning profession. So far they have fallen far short of that potential.

University-School System Alliances

School systems and universities — two learning organizations working at internal development (chapter 4), and external collaboration with each other (chapter 5). This is what will be required for the future. We have come to the same conclusion as Goodlad (1991), 'any teacher education program created or conducted without the collaboration of surrounding schools is defective' (p. 13). In post-modern society all citizens must learn to cope with the forces of change on a continuous basis. Teachers have a pivotal position, because changes are always raining down on them, and because they have to educate others to deal with change.

Implicit up to this point in this chapter is the teacher education continuum of learning. There is much to learn and keep on learning under conditions of dynamic complexity, so the whole career is a change proposition. The first five years of teaching are especially critical for laying the foundation for continuous learning (or stagnation).

Teacher development and institutional development (of universities and schools) must go hand in hand. You can't have one without the other. If there was ever a symbiotic relationship that makes complete sense it is the collaboration of universities and school systems in the initial and ongoing development of educators. The cultures of course differ (part of the definition of symbiosis). I spoke earlier of 'ready, fire, aim'. On their worst days schools are 'fire, fire, fire', and universities are 'ready, ready, ready'. But they do and are increasingly coming together to create more powerful, and sustained learning communities for student teachers, beginning teachers, teachers of longer standing, and university professors. This is one case where synergy can be achieved. Well designed field-based teacher education programs benefit mentors as much as neophytes, university professors as much as teachers.

When all is said and done, reform in teacher education must begin simultaneously in schools and in faculties of education, both independently (because one can't wait for the other) and together through multi-year alliances (which serve to put pressure and support on both institutions to change their ways and realize their relationship to each other).

There are three aspects of the new work on university-school alliances that I will take up: the concept of partnerships (using our Learning Consortium as an example); professional development schools (PDS); and teacher leadership and mentoring. Good projects incorporate all three components, but they bear separate consideration as well.

The Concept of University-School System Partnerships: The Learning Consortium

The Learning Consortium is a long-term partnership (renewable three year terms), entering its sixth year as of July 1993, involving four school districts and two higher education institutions in and around Metropolitan Toronto, Canada. The districts are large: Durham Board of Education has 55,000 students; Halton, 44,000; North York, 59,000; Scarborough, 75,000. Altogether there are 500 schools and 13,700 teachers in the Consortium boards. The two higher education institutions are also sizeable; The Faculty of Education, University of Toronto, has some ninety faculty, 1100 pre-service teachers, and 5000 in-service teachers; the Ontario Institute for Studies in Education has 140 faculty and over 2300 part and full-time graduate students.

The aim of the Consortium is to improve the quality of education for students in schools and universities by focussing on teacher development, school development, and the restructuring of districts and the faculty of education to support improvement on a continuous basis. The Consortium has three core objectives:

- to plan and initiate new programs in teacher development and school improvement;
- to generate knowledge through documenting and researching these initiatives;
- to disseminate what we are learning about teacher development and school improvement.

While the basic assumptions and objectives were broadly stated, we were committed to launching specific initiatives to realize our aims. We began in 1988 with an emphasis on cooperative learning, a theme which provided a concrete point of departure. By year three, summer and winter institutes on cooperative learning and follow through support were well established; a new field-based teacher certification program was in place; dissemination conferences and in-service were carried out on such collaborative approaches as mentoring, induction, peer coaching and school improvement planning. The Consortium partners attempted to link these activities by paying attention to consistent themes such as: teaching as career-long learning; fostering collaborative cultures; focussing on instruction. One of the frameworks we developed to describe the work at the school level links 'classroom improvement' and 'school improvement' with the 'teacher-as-learner' as the linchpin (see Fullan, Bennet and Rolheiser-Bennett, 1990).

Some of the key areas of impact of the Consortium include: extensive implementation of cooperative learning and an internal cadre in each district to keep it going; support programs for beginning teachers; the development of collaborative schools with a focus on continually expanding the instructional repertoire and effectiveness of teachers; coordination and synergy of school level and district level developments; successful leadership training for school teams, teacher leaders and administrators; new teacher preparation pilot projects that work with cohorts of thirty student teachers, placing them in small groups in collaborative schools, and coordinating the efforts of faculty of education and school staff for professional development for all involved; and, parallel changes in the structure and culture of the faculty of education and its programs (see Cullen, 1992; Fullan, in press; Lacey, 1991; and Watson and Fullan, 1992).

Through its commitment to inquiry, evaluation and dissemination, Consortium members have written many published articles, made conference presentations, conducted workshops, and received numerous visitors from many other provinces and countries. In addition, much research and evaluation is conducted by external investigators either through evaluation contracts, or through studies by graduate students, professors, and visiting educators.

Finally, it is significant that the Consortium runs virtually without outside funds. Each partner contributes $20,000 annually to generate a base budget of $120,000, which supports the secretariat and targeted evaluation and consultation. Most activities, such as the institutes, are funded directly by the participating institutions through staff development budgets. The Consortium also generates some money through conferences, workshops and consulting, which provides valuable marginal funds. More and more, externally-funded projects are being sought to enable further work to be done. The fact remains, however, that the Consortium is not seen as another temporary externally-funded project, but as a normal and integral part of helping the organizations move forward.

I do not hold up the Consortium as a model to emulate. Each of the partners still has its own agendas which do not always mesh. We do not necessarily expect this particular Consortium to last forever (see chapter 5 on multiple alliances). The partner institutions, however, are in it for the long haul — a minimum of six years in the Consortium, and a commitment to establishing learning systems with whomever they are working.

Many other jurisdictions have established similar arrangements, some of which have been mentioned earlier in the chapter. Goodlad has done as much as anyone in clarifying the concept and conditions for success and in establishing consortia partnerships between school districts and universities (Goodlad, 1988 and 1991).

These early attempts at university-school system consortia partnerships, including our own Consortium, are not yet comprehensive. As we and others proceed, these efforts are becoming deeper, i.e., they are pushing toward more radical changes in restructuring the entire teacher education continuum and the working conditions and cultures at both university and school levels. And more and more institutions have decided to try this way of working. At this larger scale we can expect the forces of inertia to be considerable. Winitzky, Stoddart and O'Keefe (1992) summarize their concerns in establishing school-university partnerships:

1 Although partnerships have often been advocated, the literature that has accumulated to guide such reform is quite limited. We know little about what works, what does not, and why.

2 Previous reforms may have been overly top-down, and the

people expected to carry them out may not have been sufficiently involved in designing them.

3 Previous reforms failed to take a systems view of education. Pressure from one part of the system may interfere with change in another part; lack of support from one may result in the withering of change in another.

4 A gulf exists between teachers' and professors' views on teaching, learning, and teacher education; this gulf is so large that they often work at cross-purposes.

5 The reward structures in both schools and universities mitigate against collaborative efforts. (p. 9)

Rudduck (1992) based on her experiences in England, calls the enterprise 'les liaisons dangereuses'. She concludes that the success of such partnerships will depend on:

- the readiness of the partners to give up their traditional mythologies about each other, and learn to respect each other's strengths and recognize each other's needs and conditions for professional survival;
- building a shared commitment to well-judged change, to exploring alternatives and to pushing back the limits of possibility in learning;
- building a shared commitment to clarifying principles and purposes, and to understanding the social and political contexts in which those purposes and principles are set to work;
- accepting a shared perception of teaching as one of the 'impossible professions' — impossible because it has 'ideas which admit no easy realization, (and) goals that are often multiple, ambiguous and conflicting;
- recognizing that the pace of worthwhile change — change that achieves new cultural coherence and significance — is relatively slow and that ways have to be found of keeping up the momentum.

A tall order for busy people, as those involved in the ever increasing Professional Development Schools movement are finding.

Professional Development Schools (PDS)

Longstanding concerns about the inadequacy of teacher education (from initial preparation to the end of the career), and the isolationist culture of schools have led to various attempts to improve both components, but rarely in conjunction. Put positively, new emphasis on teacher-as-learner, and on collaborative work cultures have converged in the concept of Professional Development Schools (PDS). Stoddart, Winitzky, and O'Keefe (1992) summarize the Holmes Group's (1990) definition:

> a Professional Development School (PDS) is a school in which university faculty work collaboratively with practitioners over time with the goal of improving teaching and learning through: (1) upgrading the education of pre-service teachers, (2) providing professional development for experienced teachers, and (3) field-based research. Inherent in the PDS model is the notion of school sites evolving as models of excellence and centers of inquiry through collaboration between school and university faculties over time. (p. 2)

In principle, then, PDS is a model that is on the right track in promising to produce learning educators and learning organizations through school-university partnerships. There are three main observations that can be made at this early stage of its development: the concept is ambitious and vague; little research data are available as yet; and the university side of the partnership is underdeveloped.

First, as to the ambitiousness and vagueness of the concept, the idea is that collaborative groups would develop the particular programs within the broad principles of the model.

Second, little evaluative data are available as the first published reports of PDS are just beginning to appear. These take on considerable importance given the ambiguity of what the model might look like in practice. Grossman (1992), for example, reports on a case study of a PDS at Lark Creek Middle School as part of the Puget Sound Professional Development Center (PSPDC) in Washington State, US. The PSPDC program places small groups of student teachers at the school for extended periods of time under the supervision of teams of mentor teachers. This field experience is inquiry oriented, and linked to a core team-taught seminar which attempts to integrate theory and practice. An extensive professional development program for experienced teachers is also undertaken which includes professors of education spending blocks or regular amounts of time at the school (see Grossman, 1992, for more details).

Lark Creek is a good example of the difficulties and potential involved in establishing a PDS. One problem common to both schools and universities is whether PDS is just another project versus whether it becomes a more integrating new way of life. One sees this dilemma at Lark Creek which was already heavily involved in a high profile state-sponsored school renewal program called 'A School for the Twenty-first Century', when a decision was taken to also become a PDS. Grossman calls this a 'dual agenda': 'From its very inception as a professional development school (Lark Creek) would be pursuing a dual agenda — to restructure itself in accordance with the goals of outcome-based education, as proposed in the twenty-first century grant, and to transform itself into a site for the career-long professional development, with a special emphasis on the preparation of preservice teachers' (p. 6).

These two programs, of course, are not in principle mutually exclusive — a point that the school principal stresses. But teachers, partly because they are not used to linking particular programs to larger concepts (and do not have time to do so), and partly because of the 'projectitis' decision-making patterns of school systems, usually experience overload and fragmentation. As observed by Grossman (1992): 'the teachers' feelings of being overwhelmed by change efforts reflects their sense of fragmentation, rather than progression towards a single coherent goal' (p. 33). Despite these problems most teachers intuitively feel and sometimes experience first hand the great potential of the new model for preparing new teachers, and for revitalizing themselves.

Third, on the university side of the partnership, the issues are both understudied, and underdeveloped. Most accounts of PDSs — even though the models are based on purportedly equal school-university collaborations — only focus on the school side of the relationship. When they do mention the university it is usually to indicate that not much impact has yet been made. In Grossman's words:

> Change has been no easier, and perhaps even more difficult, on the university side of the equation. From its inception, the professional development center has been cast as the on-going concern of relatively few faculty, rather than the responsibility of the college as a whole, despite the efforts of the dean to change this perception. The PSPDC has been seen as simply another project, rather than an effort to change the way the college does business. (*ibid*, p. 32)

In short, issues related to the *internal transformation of universities as institutions* receive little attention in the literature.

These three main problems — the vagueness of the PDS concept, the limited knowledge we have about PDS practice alongside the problems of projectitis and culture change in schools, and the lack of attention and difficulties of bringing about change in the culture and practices of universities — are evident in other studies of PDS schools. Pugach and Pasch (1992), and Jett-Simpson, Pugach and Whipp (1992) stress that a multi-year effort is required — one which focusses on complete reform. They argue 'that the work of preservice education, staff development, and school restructuring must be viewed as inseparable components of the same work' (Pugach and Pasch, 1992, p. 22). They also make the case that establishing PDSs in 'difficult' urban sites is needed, both because of the greater needs there, and because more will be learned about how to improve education.

In sum, Professional Development Schools must be assessed on how well they establish learning conditions for all educators, not the least of which is to effect changes in the cultures of schools *and* colleges of education.

Teacher Leadership and Mentoring

I have talked about the new work of the principal which among other things is to broaden the leadership capacity of the school (chapter 4). Teacher leadership — mentors, peer coaches, staff developers at the school level, curricular resource teachers, divisional and department heads, site-based planning members etc. — thus extends leadership beyond the principal. In the same way that teacher leadership extends the capacity of the school beyond the principalship, its role should be to help create the conditions and capacity for every teacher to become a leader. It sounds ideal, but teaching will not become a learning profession until the vast majority of its members become (in my terms) change agents capable of working on their own sense of purpose, through inquiry, competence building, and collaboration (chapter 2). The good news is that there has been a proliferation of leadership roles and expectations. The further good news is that these new developments have brought to the fore the new skills that teacher leaders (and ultimately all teachers) will need, but do not now possess.

Teacher-leaders face dilemmas as well as expanded opportunities. In *The New Meaning of Educational Change*, we summarized some of these issues:

Many teacher-leader roles end up distancing those in the roles from other teachers. In a study of those in teacher-leadership

roles, Smylie and Denny (1989) found that teacher-leaders consistently identified their roles in terms of helping and supporting fellow teachers in working with students and in improving
practice, but actually spent most of their time attending meetings
and 'participating in various planning and decision-making
activities at the district and building levels related to curricular,
instructional, and staff development programs'. (p. 8)

Similarly, teachers engaged in curriculum development or otherwise involved in content innovations must put their advocacy
in perspective. If these teachers try to sell a product without
recognizing that it may not be the most important thing on
other teachers' minds, and without being sensitive to the need
for other teachers to come to grips with the sense of the innovation, they will be doing exactly what most developers or
advocates of change do — confusing the change with the change
process. It is this tendency that led me to form the proposition
that the more an advocate is committed to a particular innovation, the *less* likely he or she is to be effective in getting it
implemented. The reverse is not true: Commitment is needed,
but it must be balanced with the knowledge that people may be
at different starting points, with different legitimate priorities,
and that the change process may very well result in transformation or variatons in the change. If the teacher as advocate can
become skilled at integrating the change and the change process,
he or she can become one of the most powerful forces of change.
Teachers working with other teachers at the school and classroom levels is a necessary condition for improving practice. At
least, such a development offers some potential for not only
improving classroom practice but also remedying some of the
burnout, alienation, and routine that blights the working day
of many teachers. (Fullan and Stiegelbauer, 1991, pp. 138–9)

I have said that the teachers' backgrounds do not prepare them for
these collaborative leadership roles, and that such preparation must
begin in the pre-service program. Once teachers are in leadership
positions their lack of preparation for these roles become self-evident.
Manthei's (1992) research found that 'most of the aspiring mentor
teachers want, but after years of successful teaching do not possess, the
knowledge and skills to create and/or assume new teacher leadership
roles' (p. 1). Manthei gathered data from teachers taking mentor teacher
preparation courses. The ratings for knowledge and skills most needed

by mentors (and least possessed) were: application of adult development and learning concepts, and reflective conferencing and observing
skills. Even lower was 'knowledge of organizational issues'. Says
Manthei, the data show 'how little the experienced teachers know about
their institutional structures and processes, even those related to the
area of mentoring where they have expressed interest and shown
initiative' (p. 14). Studies do consistently report that teacher leaders
learn a great deal from their experiences in these roles, evidently less
because they are prepared and more because it represents such a novel
learning experience.

Wasley's (1991) detailed case studies of three teacher-leaders cor-
roborates that teachers normally do not have the opportunity to develop
the skills needed for leadership roles, but she makes a more fundamental point: that such roles cannot succeed unless they are part and parcel
of a larger contextual change in redefining the roles and incentives for
all teachers. The importance of context in determining whether a given
program will be substantial or superficial is clearly found in Feiman-
Nemser and Parker's (1992) comparison of two US mentoring programs
for beginning teachers. These authors found a world of difference in
the Los Angeles and the Albuquerque initiatives.

In Los Angeles, the mentors teach full-time and 'fit their mentoring
in and around the edges' (p. 3) compared to Albuquerque where the
mentors are released full-time to work with interns (made possible by
a special program that places interns in classrooms as part of a master's
program, thereby freeing up regular positions). Relative to selection
criteria, the Los Angeles process is bureaucratic with an emphasis on
the mentor's own classroom performance, while the Albuquerque
process is more qualitative stressing qualities as 'leader, learner, and
member of a team' (p. 7).

In preparing for the role Los Angeles mentors participate in a
front-end workshop, but 'received little help integrating the variety of
information and ideas they are exposed to with the actual demands and
requirements of their work' (p. 8). By contrast, 'in Albuquerque, support teachers learn about their work by doing it. Aside from a weeklong
orientation (at the beginning), most of the preparation that support
teachers receive continues throughout the school year' (p. 8). Overall,
Los Angeles mentors function as 'local guides' helping novices get
comfortable with the job compared to Albuquerque mentors who serve
as 'educational companions' focussing on clinical support and the
improvement of instructional practice.

Feiman-Nemser and Parker (1992) conclude that the Albuquerque
program is far more substantial as it impacts on the culture of teaching:

When mentors act as agents of cultural change, they seek to break down the traditional isolation among teachers by fostering norms of collaboration and shared inquiry. They build networks with novices and their colleagues. They create opportunities for teachers to visit each other's classrooms. They facilitate conversations among teachers about teaching. (p. 17)

Two programs, going under the same label of mentoring, as different as night and day.

The New Work of Teacher Unions

In some of the new work of teacher unions, we are beginning to see both a positive thrust to reforming teaching, and a more boundary-free networking of teachers as learners. The American Federation of Teachers (AFT) has been active in forging reform alliances between unions and districts, and in its 'Educational Research and Dissemination' program (Shanker, 1990). The School Renewal Network of the National Education Association (NEA) represents another substantial initiative (Watts and Castle, 1992). Using electronic networking and periodic face-to-face meetings, 'dialogic networks' are designed 'to allow a community of users to carry on a discussion or participate in a conference with all members of the community' on particular topics over a period of time (p. 685). Not without implementation problems (and a corresponding need to know how to set-up and facilitate the exchanges), Watts and Castle report several positive outcomes: increased teacher professionalism, increased dialogue between researchers and practitioners, greater possibility of substantive change through the use of information, breaking down of institutional and hierarchical barriers, and eliminating barriers of time and place. Ultimately, according to Watts and Castle, 'these networks have the power to change not only the user but the environment in which the user works' (p. 685).

A similar initiative by the Ontario Teachers' Federation (OTF, 1992b) funded by the Ontario government is just getting underway. Appropriately called 'Creating a Culture of Change' the project focusses on teacher-driven changes in 'the transition years' (grades 7, 8 and 9), but is not exclusive to teachers at these levels. The project is expressly aimed at supporting and stimulating teachers to make changes in curriculum and teaching through inservice collaboration among teachers, and with other agencies. The OTF/Ministry of Education initiative 'is founded on the belief that real educational change occurs when teachers understand the need for change and actively seek solutions to the problems of teaching and learning' (*ibid*, p. 1).

Lieberman and McLaughlin (1992) discuss the 'power and problems' of these new networking strategies:

> Networks offer a way for teachers to experience growth in their careers through deepened and expanded classroom expertise and new leadership roles . . . (They) provide teachers with the motivation to challenge existing practices and to grow professionally. (pp. 674–5)

Successful networks, they say, share common features: focus, variety, discourse communities, and leadership opportunities. The problems according to Lieberman and McLaughlin include: questions about quality, difficulty of applications in the classroom and school, instability over time, overextension, ownership, enlarging teachers' views of their roles, leadership of networks, evaluation, and the accommodation of legitimate external goals (to the network).

The potential of these teacher-driven strategies for change in terms of the themes of this book should be obvious: they focus on building a community of teacher-learners from the ground up. To the extent that they create a new culture of learners, structural changes will follow. To restructure is not to reculture, but to reculture is to restructure. The question marks are: what about teachers who show no interest? And, will teacher unions be able to form productive alliances with other agencies — schools as organizations, districts, businesses, universities, and the like? Partnerships are essential since no one group can make a difference on its own. But above all, and most significantly, these strategies represent another change force pushing toward 'breakpoint' in creating a new learning culture in the profession of teaching (Land and Jarman, 1992; and chapter 7). Substantial change will not take place until everyday teachers start talking about it, and doing something about it.

Putting it Together

The question is how seriously is society — and those in educational institutions — going to take the preparation and continuous development of teachers. We cannot have a learning society without a learning profession of teachers. Although comparisons with Japanese and Chinese education are overdrawn it is instructive to consider how these Asian countries treat induction into the profession.

In China, because of the sheer size of numbers there are no doubt many weak beginnings to the career. This problem notwithstanding, Liping Ma's dialogue with Yu Yi (a high school principal with forty years of experience) is revealing (Yi and Ma, 1992). First, it is significant that Yi, as principal, sees teacher education as an obligation of the school:

> Formal teacher education conducted in special institutions can only accomplish half the task of teacher preparation; the rest of it must be achieved in schools where people really teach. In addition, since teaching is a life-long career in China, teacher education and teachers' self-education should never stop. (p. 7)

Schools take responsibility for training beginning teachers using a minimum three-year apprenticeship program:

> It takes time to make a mature teacher. Some schools have a three-year on the job training program to help beginning teachers. We decided to let our program last five years. (p. 9)

In Yi's case, a three-fold purpose is pursued with beginning teachers: (i) to let new teachers know the value of teaching as a career and to expose them to concrete examples of good teachers (in literature as well as in practice); (ii) to instill the notion that 'the most important disposition of a good teacher is to keep on pursuing new learning and improving yourself' (p. 13); and (iii) 'to develop particular skills and routine' (p. 14).

Stevenson and Stigler's (1992) systematic study of schooling in Chinese, Japanese and US societies is even more enlightening. They found that the number one reason for becoming a teacher in all three cultures was the desire to work with children and adolescents (moral purpose). After that, differences begin to set in mostly around skill and know-how, and how to acquire the latter on a continuous basis. After recounting the inadequacies of US teacher education (at college and especially its absence on the job), Stevenson and Stigler have this to say:

> In Japan, the system of teacher training is much like an apprenticeship. There is a systematic effort to pass on the accumulated wisdom of teaching practice to each new generation of teachers and to keep perfecting that kind of practice by providing for the continuing professional interaction of teachers. The teacher's

first year of employment marks the beginning of a lengthy and elaborate process. By Japanese law, beginning teachers must receive a minimum of twenty days of in-service training during their first year on the job. Supervising this training are master teachers, selected for their teaching ability and their willingness to assist their young colleagues. During one-year leaves of absence from their own classrooms, they spend their days observing beginning teachers, offering suggestions for improvement, and counselling them about effective teaching techniques.

In addition, Japanese teachers, beginners as well as seasoned teachers, are required to perfect their teaching skills through interaction with other teachers. For instance, meetings are organized by the vice-principal and head teachers at their school. These experienced professionals assume responsibility for advising and guiding their young colleagues. The head teachers also organize meetings to discuss teaching techniques and to devise lesson plans and handouts. These discussions are very pragmatic and are aimed both at developing better teaching techniques and at constructing plans for specific lessons. A whole meeting might be devoted to the most effective ways to phrase questions about a topic or the most absorbing ways of capturing children's interest in a lesson. Meetings at each school are supplemented by informal district-wide study groups and by courses at municipal or prefectural education centers. . . .

Opportunities to learn from other teachers are influenced, in part, by the physical arrangements of the schools. In Japanese and Chinese schools, a large room in each school is designed as a teachers' room, and each teacher is assigned a desk in this room. Here they spend their time away from the classroom preparing lessons, correcting students' papers, and discussing teaching techniques. American teachers, isolated in their own classrooms, find it much harder to discuss their work with colleagues. Their desks and teaching materials are in their own classrooms, and the only common space available to teachers is usually a cramped room that often houses supplies and the school's duplicating facilities, along with a few chairs and a coffee machine. (pp. 159–61)

Japanese and Chinese teachers have larger class sizes (forty-five), but they also have less time that is classroom-bound (maximum of three-four hours a day). It is not simply time available that counts here, but *the professional norms* governing how that time is used: 'time is freed up for teachers to meet and work together on a daily basis, to prepare lessons for the next day, to work with individual children and to attend staff meetings' (p. 164). This two-way commitment between society and its teachers is also reflected in the longer hours Chinese and Japanese teachers spend at school each day (over nine hours compared to a little over seven hours in the US in Stevenson and Stigler's findings). Of course, both expectations and working conditions in Asian schools are more conducive to spending time at school productively.

There are other differences. More emphasis is placed in Asia on teachers' skilled performance, clarity and know how. Student discipline is less of a problem because the school and parents spend more time on entry into the 'social environment' of schooling, and on peer and group relationships.

No other culture can or should be 'borrowed', and we can quarrel over some of the content and side-effects of Asian education. The underlying message for teaching as a profession, however, should not be missed: Westerners are not convinced that teaching 'should be one of our most esteemed professions' (p. 172). Teacher education and teaching is not now a learning system where people get better as a result of learning from each other and attempting to perfect their craft.

Working backwards from the skills and dispositions that will be required by students and citizens in learning societies, we see what is needed in schools as learning organizations (chapter 4). The quality of these organizations depends on reform in teacher education which must drive and be driven by new conceptions of teaching as a skilled, morally committed learning profession. New developments in school-university-teacher union partnerships which encompass *changes in the cultures* of schools, universities, and teacher organizations are in the right direction, but currently represent weak manifestations of what will be needed. We must not allow superficial attempts that use only the labels of partnerships, restructuring, mentoring, and the like. The weakest and potentially strongest link in educational reform right now is the initial preparation, and on the job development of educators. So far western societies have not been able to bring themselves to take the challenge of reforming teacher education seriously. Yet, *'no other change is as basic as this one'* (Stevenson and Stigler, 1992, p. 173, my emphasis).

Chapter 7

The Individual and the Learning Society

It may be those who do most, dream most.

Stephen Leacock

I focus on the individual for two reasons. First, external events are always happening to individuals whether they like it or not, so ability to manage change is an essential skill in post-modern society. Change is mandatory, growth is optional (Laing, 1992). Thus, we do not have a choice between change and non-change, but we do have a choice about how we respond. Second, focussing on the individual is not a substitute for system change, *it is the most effective strategy for accomplishing it.*

The ideas in this book culminate in several powerful themes. The ultimate aim of education is to produce a learning society, indeed a learning globe. The key to learning is the teacher who must combine continuous inner and outer learning. Moral purpose and change agentry — caring and competence — are intimate partners. Neither equity nor excellence by themselves get us anywhere. They must feed on each other. Finally, teachers more than most people are in a privileged position to pursue the meaning of life through the merging of microcosm and macrocosm.

The Learning Society: Student Cum Citizen

Education, knowledge and learning are the issues of the day. Says Drucker (1992): 'the center of gravity has shifted to the knowledge worker' (p. 5); 'every enterprise has to become a learning institution (and) a teaching institution (p. 108). Organizations (and societies) that build in continuous learning and continuous teaching in jobs at all levels will dominate the twenty-first century, claims Drucker.

We know increasingly more about what learning should focus on, and how people learn. The necessary combination of intellectual development (such as Gardner's (1992) 'education for understanding'), and social development (such as cooperative learning's emphasis on learning to work in groups) is becoming more evident. The abilities to think and present ideas on the one hand, and to work with others on the other hand are being recognized by education and businesses alike as central to the world's future. Permeating these twin purposes is a third purpose — the positive disposition to keep on learning in the face of constant change and societal complexity. Put another way, the ability to cope with change, learning as much as possible with each encounter is the generic capacity needed for the twenty-first century.

What we don't know is how to achieve these goals for *all* students locally, let alone nationally and internationally. The reason that this is difficult is that it requires a prodigious and mobilized effort and collaboration among a number of constituencies — parents and community, business and industry (labour and management), government and other social agencies, and the education system. The education system cannot do it alone, but it must help break the cycle of disjuncture by helping to lead the way in its own right and through alliances.

The development of a learning society is a societal quest, not just because education cannot do it alone, but because we are talking about a learning *society* not just a learning school system. The commitment and practice of learning must find itself in all kinds of organizations and institutions if it is to achieve any kind of force in society as a whole.

The Canadian Institute of Advanced Research's (CIAR, 1992) program for *The Learning Society* puts the challenge most clearly. The social environment in early life begins to shape the development of competence and coping skills; schools are not set up to deal with these differences, and if anything widen the gap between the haves and the have-nots; businesses, social agencies and other institutions either make it worse, do little to reverse the problem, or find that it is too late. The rapidity of technological, demographic, and social changes puts even greater pressure on individuals to cope. Those least equipped get further and further behind, becoming both liabilities to themselves and society. Human development is both social and economic, both individual and societal.

A central challenge stated in the CIAR proposal 'is to define the relationship between individual and collective development, and to enhance our understanding of their fundamental interdependency' (p. 20). Moreover, they observe, 'just as the need for our society for informed, skilled, and compassionate citizens is increasing, the actual capacity of our society to meet this need appears to be on the wane' (p. 22).

CIAR's proposal for action makes it clear that we must look worldwide for ideas, and ultimately look worldwide for solutions:

> The project we propose begins in this urgent context. We do not believe that there is an easy solution to any of these problems. Nor do we believe, however, that the problems are the inevitable consequence of life in the modern era. If one takes a cross-national perspective, one discovers that certain societies are adapting far more successfully to the requirements of the information age than the others. Moreover, the societies that appear to be adapting most successfully are those that have historically placed a very high value on learning, and regard it as a lifelong process. Not coincidentally, they are also societies that invest heavily in mothers and children, that have a highly educated work force, and whose social institutions ensure that learning takes place across all social classes, and across the full life span. Rather than experiencing an erosion of the family and other basic social institutions, then, certain modern nations have actually managed to revitalize them, and dedicate themselves to the new and more technical demands of the modern era.
>
> What we propose to do in the present project is to develop a profile of what 'a learning society' must be like, if it is to thrive in the modern era. Our attack on this problem will be three-pronged. (1) We will examine the way in which learning and development are fostered in societies where the transition to the modern era is being negotiated most successfully. (2) We will examine the barriers to such development that exist in our own society, with special emphasis on factors leading to emotional, behavioral, or academic problems in our children, but with additional emphasis on barriers to continuous learning and development throughout the life span. In addition, critical aspects that lead to successful development within our societal context will also receive special attention. (3) We will consider the problem of getting there from here. That is to say, we will consider the problem of re-vitalizing and/or modifying our own institutions, in a fashion that will more successfully meet the needs of our society across the life span, in a human and

humane fashion. Included in this consideration is an explicit
recognition that such adaptations may require rethinking the
nature of the collective commitment between individuals and
the societies that they comprise. (pp. 22–3)

In short, the development of a learning society is all of our responsibilities: 'if we are to find a way to optimize the development of our
human resources, we must examine the nature of our social institutions
throughout the lifespan, and determine the extent to which they do or
do not foster a lifetime of continuous learning and the ability to cope
with change' (CIAR, 1992, p. 43). Is it too much to ask that educators,
given that they are in the learning business, would help lead the way?
Even if they are not being appreciated in the early stages.

The Teacher as Key: Inner and Outer Learning

The pursuit of *planned* changed is a mug's game, because reality under
conditions of dynamic complexity is fundamentally non-linear. Most
change is unplanned. We need to recognize this first, and take advantage
of it by developing our inner and outer learning capacities. These
capacities apply to all of us, but especially to teachers. It seems obvious
to say, except that we don't practise it, that you can't have a learning
society without learning students, and you can't have learning students
without learning teachers. Inner learning (intrapersonal sense-making)
and outer learning (relating and collaborating with others) run together,
but they are also separable.

Inner Learning

Teachers (and all of us) should think of change and innovation as they
would about their own lives. Life (and change) is not always moving
forward, bad things happen beyond our control, fortune shines on
us unexpectedly etc., etc. That is life. But, and this is the key, some
people cope better and even thrive, while others fall apart. The very
first place to begin the change process is within ourselves. In complex
societies like our own, we have to learn to cope and grow despite the
system. It is not that the system is out to get us (sometimes that is
the case), but that it (as it changes in dynamically complex ways) is
indifferent to our purposes. Therefore, teachers should look for their
first lessons from individuals who do a better job of learning even
under adverse circumstances.

Csikszentmihalyi's (1990) analysis of *Flow* and optimal experience is a good place to start. He observes: 'In each person's life, the chances of only good things happening are extremely slim' (p. 202). Earlier he sets the stage:

> The primary reason it is so difficult to achieve happiness centers on the fact that, contrary to the myths mankind has developed to reassure itself, the universe was not created to answer our needs. Frustration is deeply woven into the fabric of life. (*ibid*, p. 7)

Csikszentmihalyi argues that you cannot find happiness by seeking only to change the external conditions of life. It is 'people who learn to control inner experiences (who) will be able to determine the quality of their lives' (*ibid*, p. 2). Moreover, those who try to make life better for everyone without having learned to control their own lives first usually end up making matters worse all around (p. 191). In his chapter on 'cheating chaos' Csikszentmihalyi's analysis of the four traits of the autotelic self ('a self that has self-contained goals') comes very close to describing the ideal change agent:

(i) Setting goals.
(ii) Becoming immersed in the activity.
(iii) Paying attention to what is happening, and
(iv) Learning to enjoy immediate experience (*ibid*, pp. 209–13).

It is not a fixed path because 'paying attention to what is happening' means taking change into account: 'The focus is still set by the person's goal, but it is open enough to notice and adapt to external events' (*ibid*, p. 205). According to Csikszentmihalyi, 'the outcome of having an autotelic self — of learning to set goals, to develop skills, to be sensitive to feedback, to know how to concentrate and get involved — is that one can enjoy life even when objective circumstances are brutish and nasty' (*ibid*, pp. 212–3).

Teachers more than anyone should be autotelic, not looking for clarity and meaning *in* the latest innovation or set of educational policies. Over any given period of time, innovations and systems are not *objectively coherent*. We must work out our meaning: 'subjective experience is not just one of the dimensions of life, it *is* life itself' (*ibid*, p. 192). With all the emphasis on collegiality and collaboration, it is easy to neglect the necessity of learning to think for oneself. The capacity to think and work independently is essential to educational reform. The psychologist Anthony Storr (1988) makes this case well in his

analysis of the power and necessity of *solitude*. Interpersonal relationships, he argues, do not constitute the only path toward personal
fulfillment. The capacity to be alone is a sign of great emotional
maturity, 'linked with self-discovery and self-realization; with becoming aware of our deepest needs, feelings and impulses' (p. 21).

Storr also shows how solitude can be a source of personal meaning
and creativity. New personal meaning is at the heart of successful
innovation, especially under circumstances of frequent change:

> The capacity to be alone is a valuable resource when changes
> of mental attitude are required. After major alterations in cir-
> cumstances, fundamental reappraisal of the significance and
> meaning of existence may be needed. In a culture in which
> interpersonal relationships are generally considered to provide
> the answer to every form of distress, it is sometimes difficult
> to persuade well-meaning helpers that solitude can be as thera-
> peutic as emotional support. (*ibid*, p. 29)

And,

> Learning, thinking, innovation, and maintaining contact with
> one's own inner world are all facilitated by solitude. (*ibid*, p. 28)

Thus, sorting out one's own individual stance toward improvement is just as important as deciding on collective responses. I don't
want to overstate the case for personal change. Individuals don't have
limitless energy to deal with adverse circumstances. Some circumstances
are intolerable and must be attacked directly. But fundamentally we
must take a different tack in dealing with the barrage of expected and
unexpected changes. Paradox is standard fare in the complexity of
change processes, and it shows itself here in the realization that *personal
change is the most powerful route to system change.* In *Prisons We Choose to
Live Inside*, Lessing (1986) says, 'it is my belief that it is the individual,
in the long run, who will set the tone, provide the real development
in society' (p. 71). One of the ten megatrends of the 1990s identified
by Naisbitt and Aberdene (1990) is 'the triumph of the individual'.
They make this powerful observation: 'Individuals today can leverage
change far more effectively than most institutions' (p. 298). Senge (1990)
sums it up:

> Organizations learn through individuals who learn. Individual
> learning does not guarantee organizational learning. But with-
> out it no organizational learning occurs. (p. 139)

A sound personal learning stance is the key both to optimal individual survival and to system change. To accomplish the latter people do of course need others.

Outer Learning

Outer learning is about connectedness. It is about Rosenholtz's (1989) or Nias *et al*'s (1992) highly collaborative school cultures, where teachers work and learn from each other on an ongoing basis. It is about Huberman's (1992) career cycle artisan who seeks ideas and skills for greater and greater mastery wherever he or she can find them, inside or outside the school. It is about Stacey's (1992) multiple cultures where people learn from diversity within the organization. It is about connecting the inner self to people as people — those around you at work, and family and social relationships outside work.

When Csikszentmihalyi (1990) talks about 'focussing attention on the world' and 'discovering new solutions', he is talking about the fact that the world is always changing, and that we better pay constant attention to it — partly because some of the best ideas are 'out there', and partly because we will not survive for long without a dialectical relationship with external events. Growth occurs when individuals or groups cope with tough, intractable problems and overcome them.

The first message of the combination of inner and outer learning is that we as individuals must take the initiative if we are to avoid becoming helpless, overloaded, dependent victims of change forces. In Csikszentmihalyi's words: 'if values and institutions no longer provide as supportive a framework as they once did, each person must use whatever tools are available to carve out a meaningful, enjoyable life' (p. 16). Don't be constrained by other people's stagnation — or by their innovations for that matter.

The second message is to realize 'the force of connecting' (Land and Jarman, 1992):

Growth, change, and ultimately evolution occur as individuals, organizations, and society increase the depth of their relationships by continually broadening and strengthening their interdependent connections. (p. 189)

The vital skill is to be able 'to build ever more connections in a varied environment' (*ibid*, p. 30).

The third message is that our connections must be more balanced, more authentic, more to the total person. In the 'total teacher' we advocated that teachers 'appreciate the total person in working with others':

> Trying to understand the people with whom we work is important for building these relationships. Appreciating the total person in our colleagues involves, by definition, both the professional and non-professional realms of life. We saw in Nias *et al*'s (1989) case studies that 'valuing individuals as people' was a strong feature of the collaborative schools. Interest in and consideration of the life circumstances of individual teachers are difficult because they mean balancing concern on the one hand, with respect for privacy on the other. Research on life-cycles, career cycles and gender factors in teaching all show how teachers' personal circumstances differ and vary over time. If we do not relate appropriately to other people, we increase the chances of conflict, alienation and mismatched responses or strategies. (Fullan and Hargreaves, 1991, pp. 74–5)

A related part of balance concerns work/family or work/non-work relationships — what Senge (1990) calls 'ending the war between work and family':

> The disciplines of the learning organization will, I believe, end the taboo that has surrounded the topic of balancing work and family, and has kept it off the corporate agenda. The learning organization cannot support personal mastery without supporting personal mastery in all aspects of life. It cannot foster shared vision without calling forth personal visions, and personal visions are always multifaceted — they always include deeply felt desires for our personal, professional, organizational, and family lives. Lastly, the artificial boundary between work and family is anathema to systems thinking. There is a natural connection between a person's work life and all other aspects of life. We live only one life, but for a long time our organizations have operated as if this simple fact could be ignored, as if we had two separate lives. (p. 307)

'One cannot build a learning organization on a foundation of broken homes and strained relationships' observes Senge (p. 312). Kaplan (1991) has the same message: people who live better lead better.

The fourth message is that the combination of personally driven inner and outer learning is the best strategy for *system change*:

> Our experience with hundreds of organizations, over a period exceeding thirty years, has led to the conclusion that *organizations and nations don't change — only individuals change.* When enough individuals believe and live the Creative Worldview, organizations and nations will also. (Land and Jarman, 1992, p. 134)

Systems change when enough kindred spirits coalesce in the same change direction. This is why top-down structural change does not work. You can't mandate what matters because there are no shortcuts to changes in systems' cultures. But like-minded people, pushing for change do add up. In commenting on the successful transformation of the Ford Motor Company in going from $3.3 billion loss in 1980–82 to 1986–87 in which profits surpassed those of General Motors for the first time since 1924, one executive put it this way: 'I believe that the most profound and lasting change occurs when the rank and file want it so badly that *they* take the initiative and manage upward' (Pascale, 1990, p. 122). It is significant too that 'learning' has been added to Ford's list of values (along with people, productivity, and profits) in its mission statement. another executive comments:

> In the last analysis, Ford's continued ability to learn and adapt depends on our philosophy of management. There has been a radical change in the company's thinking regarding the managers' role. They are viewed today as change agents and facilitators — not just as experts and controllers. If we can internalize this mindset as a way of life at Ford, we may indeed have reason to hope that we can continue to revitalize ourselves. (*ibid*, p. 173)

Fifth and finally, it is not enough to be a highly collaborative team member of a given organization. The personal capacity for inner and outer learning must be portable, because over a lifetime people will inevitably be moving from group to group, and groups themselves will experience changing membership on a continuous basis. As Csikszentmihalyi (1990) states, 'Even the most successful career, the most rewarding family relationship eventually runs dry' (p. 214). People need the capacity to form and reform productive learning relationships time and time again. The more people that have it, the more likely there will be connections that are generative of new learning experiences.

I have deliberately moved outside the educational literature to place the teacher's role as a learner in society in a wider perspective. With this broader and more fundamental conception, teachers should be in a better position to judge and act on learning opportunities. Specific strategies and techniques can be appreciated, not as step-by-step actions, but with greater overall meaning. And there are plenty of particular guidelines and ideas available such as our own twelve guidelines for teachers, which are spelled out in detail in Fullan and Hargreaves (1991):

   (i)   Locate, listen to and articulate your inner voice.
   (ii)   Practise reflection in action, on action and about action.
   (iii)   Develop a risk-taking mentality.
   (iv)   Trust processes as well as people.
   (v)   Appreciate the total person in working with others.
   (vi)   Commit to working with colleagues.
   (vii)   Seek variety and avoid balkanization.
   (viii)   Redefine your role to extend beyond the classroom.
   (ix)   Balance work and life.
   (x)   Push and support principals and other administrators to develop interactive professionalism.
   (xi)   Commit to continuous improvement and perpetual learning.
   (xii)   Monitor and strengthen the connection between your development and students' development. (p. 64)

Educators will also be able to draw more fully and critically on valuable resources like Stephen Covey's (1989) *Seven Habits of Highly Effective People*, again, not as seven steps to greatness, but as a set of ideas to help one grow, and be a positive force to those with whom one comes in contact. It is no accident that the seven habits have much in common with the themes in this book:

   (i)   The Habit of Personal Vision
   (ii)   The Habit of Personal Leadership
   (iii)   The Habit of Personal Management
   (iv)   The Habit of Interpersonal Leadership
   (v)   The Habit of Communication (seek first to understand, then to be understood)
   (vi)   The Habit of Creative Cooperation
   (vii)   The Habit of Self-Renewal

Moral Purpose and Change Agentry

Moral purpose and change agentry synergize care and competence, equity and excellence. In the teaching profession these two facets of educational development have not come together. When teachers work on personal vision-building and see how their commitment to making a difference in the classroom is connected to the wider purpose of education, it gives practical and moral meaning to their profession. When they pursue learning through constant inquiry they are practising what they preach, benefiting themselves and their students by always learning. When the Japanese teacher works and works at perfecting her lesson, she is gaining the mastery that will be needed to accomplish her moral purpose. When one teacher collaborates with another, or many teachers work in a new alliance with each other and outside partners, they are enlarging their horizons as they lengthen and strengthen the levers of improvement.

When many educators act this way systems start to change, and become the environments that prod and support further growth and development. Independent change forces intersect to produce radical breakthroughs. But it is not linear. The capacity to learn is as critical in facing setbacks as it is in celebrating successes. Ultimately, moral purpose and change agentry place the individual teacher on a different plane where one can find personal meaning in a collective enterprise.

Merging Microcosm and Macrocosm

Macrocosm is the learning society and the learning world. Microcosm is Monday morning. Teachers above all in society must have a foot in both 'cosmos' because they cannot be effective in one without being plugged into the other. Aside from religion, teaching and learning is as close to the meaning of life as one can get. From Senge's 'indivisible whole' to Land and Jarman's 'wholistic view' to Einsteins's 'widening our circle of compassion to embrace all living creatures and the whole of nature in its beauty', the role of education is a search for worldwide understanding and more complex and deeper connections and interdependencies.

When Kasuo Wada, the Japanese Yaohan International supermarket tycoon moved to Hong Kong in 1989 and became immediately successful when people fearful of its takeover by China in 1997 were leaving in droves, he was practising this philosophy. In his words:

If you think positively, then you can change your life and you have unlimited potential. And if you change, then eventually the whole world will change. There will be no boundaries within yourself, and by extrapolation eventually there will be no borders between countries. (Dikkenberg, 1992, p. 22)

Most of us are not in a position to practise this approach on such a grand scale. And there are horrible circumstances where individuals have no resources and power to fight back. But in the long run inner learning is one resource that paradoxically can alter external conditions, especially if it is linked to outer learning connections.

Csikszentmihalyi (1990) characterizes where we are in this quest as we finish the twentieth century:

In the past few thousand years — a mere split second in evolutionary time — humanity has achieved incredible advances in the *differentiation* of consciousness. We have developed a realization that mankind is separate from other forms of life. We have conceived of individual human beings as separate from one another. We have invented abstraction and analysis — the ability to separate dimensions of objects and processes from each other, such as the velocity of a falling object from its weight and its mass. It is this differentiation that has produced science, technology, and the unprecedented power of mankind to build up and to destroy its environment.

But complexity consists of *integration* as well as differentiation. The task of the next decades and centuries is to realize this under-developed component of the mind. Just as we have learned to separate ourselves from each other and from the environment, we now need to learn how to reunite ourselves with other entities around us without losing our hard-won individuality. The most promising faith for the future might be based on the realization that the entire universe is a system related by common laws and that it makes no sense to impose our dreams and desires on nature without taking them into account. Recognizing the limitations of human will, accepting a cooperative rather than a ruling role in the universe, we should feel the relief of the exile who is finally returning home. The problem of meaning will then be resolved as the individual's purpose merges with the universal flow. (pp. 239–40)

Teachers are privileged and burdened with the responsibility of helping all students become inner and outer learners who will connect to wider and wider circles of society. Teachers cannot do it alone. At this stage, they have to do it despite the system. But this is how breakthroughs occur. And they will find allies. If teachers don't force the issue nobody will be able to. The dynamically complex patterns between the microworld of making a difference in the lives of particular students, and the macroworld evolution of learning societies is the real arena of teacherdom.

References

ACKER, S. (1989) 'It's what we do already, but . . . Primary school teachers and the 1988 Education Act', paper presented to the Conference on Ethnography, Education and Policy, St. Hilda's College, Oxford.

AMERICAN RESEARCH INSTITUTE (1992) *Survey of Stressful Occupations*, Washington, DC, ARI.

AYERS, W. (1992) 'Through the looking glass: Teachers and teaching in film', paper presented at the annual meeting of the American Educational Research Association, San Francisco.

BAKER, P., CURTIS, D. and BENENSON, W. (1991) *Collaborative Opportunities to Build Better Schools*, Illinois, Illinois Association for Supervision and Curriculum Development.

BECKHARD, R. and PRITCHARD, W. (1992) *Changing the Essence*, San Francisco, CA, Jossey-Bass.

BEER, M., EISENSTAT, R. and SPECTOR, B. (1990) *The Critical Path to Corporate Renewal*, Boston, MA, Harvard Business School Press.

BERENDS, M. (1992) 'A description of restructuring in nationally nominated schools', paper presented at the annual meeting of the American Educational Research Association, San Francisco.

BLOCK, P. (1987) *The Empowered Manager*, San Francisco, CA, Jossey-Bass.

BROWN, J.S. (1991) 'Research that reinvents the corporation', *Harvard Business Review*, 69, 1, pp. 102–11.

BURBACH, H. and FIGGINS, M. (1992) 'A thematic profile of the images of teachers in film', paper presented at the annual meeting of American Educational Research Association, San Francisco.

CALDWELL, B. and SPINKS, J. (1992) *Leading the Self-managing School*, Lewes, Falmer Press.

CANADIAN INSTITUTE OF ADVANCED RESEARCH (CIAR) (1992) *The Learning Society*, Toronto, Ontario, CIAR.

CARNEGIE FORUM ON EDUCATION AND THE ECONOMY (1986) 'A nation prepared: Teachers for the twenty-first century' (Report of the Task Force on Teaching as a Profession), New York, CFEE.

CHERNISS, C. and KRANTZ, D. (1983) 'The ideological community as an antidote to burnout in the human services', in FARBER, B.A. (Ed.) *Stress and Burnout in Human Service Professions*, New York, Pergamon Press.

CHRISTENSEN, G. (1992) 'The changing role of the administrator in an accelerated school', paper presented at the annual meeting of the American Educational Research Association, San Francisco.

COHEN, D. and SPILLANE, J. (1992) 'Policy and practice: The relations between governance and instruction', in GRANT, G. (Ed.) *Review of Research in Education. American Education Research Association*, Washington, DC, AERA, pp. 3–49.

COMER, J. (1992) 'A brief history and summary of the school development program', New Haven, CT, unpublished paper.

COMER, J. and HAYNES, N. (1992) 'Summary of school development program (SDP) effects', New Haven, CT, unpublished paper.

CORBETT, H.K. and WILSON, B. (1990) *Testing Reform and Rebellion*, Norwood, NY, Ablex.

COVEY, S. (1989) *The Seven Habits of Highly Effective People*, New York, Simon & Schuster.

COX, P. and DEFREES, J. (1991) 'Work in progress: Restructuring in ten Maine schools', prepared for the Maine Department of Education, US.

CRM FILMS (1991) *Groupthink*, Carlsbad, CA, CRM.

CSIKSZENTMIHALYI, M. (1990) *Flow: The Psychology of Optimal Experience*, New York, NY, Harper Collins Publisher.

CULLEN, E. (1992) 'The Learning Consortium Annual Report: Year Four', Toronto, Ontario, unpublished.

DALIN, P. and ROLFF, H.-G. (1992) *Changing the School Culture*, Oslo, Norway, International Management for Training in Educational Change.

DARESH, J. and PLAYKO, M. (1992) *The Professional Development of School Administrators*, Boston, MA, Allyn & Bacon.

DARLING-HAMMOND, L. and ASCHER, C. (1992) *Creating Accountability in Big City Schools*, New York, NY, ERIC Clearinghouse on Urban Education.

DAVIES, A. (1989) *The Human Element*, Harmondsworth, UK, Penguin.

DEPARTMENT OF EDUCATION AND SCIENCE (1992) *Reform of Initial Teacher Training*, London, Department of Education and Science.

DIKKENBERG, J. (1992) 'Positively optimistic', *Asia Magazine*, 30, 22, p. 22.

DRUCKER, P. (1992) *Managing the Future*, New York, Dutton.

DRUMMOND, W. and ANDREWS, T. (1980) 'The influence of federal and state governments on teacher education', *Phi Delta Kappan*, 62, 2, pp. 97–9.

DURHAM COUNTY BOARD OF EDUCATION AND FACULTY OF EDUCATION, UNIVERSITY OF TORONTO (1992) *Making Changes at Brock High School*, Video, Oshawa, Ontario, Durham Board of Education.

EASTON, J. (1991) *Decision Making and School Improvement: LSCs in the First Two Years Reform*, Chicago, IL, Chicago Panel on Public School Policy and Finance.

EDUCATION WEEK (1991) 'Winning designs for a new generation of winning schools', Washington, DC.

ELMORE, R. (1990) *Restructuring Schools*, San Francisco, CA, Jossey-Bass.

ELMORE, R. (1992) 'The role of local school districts in instructional improvement', paper presented at the annual meeting of the American Educational Research Association, San Francisco.

EVANS, J. (1992) 'Foundation chair reflects on challenges for the future', *Grantors' Memo*, 8, 8. Toronto, Gordon Foundation.

FACULTY OF EDUCATION, UNIVERSITY OF TORONTO (1992a) *Making a Difference*, video, Toronto, Ontario.

FACULTY OF EDUCATION, UNIVERSITY OF TORONTO (1992b) *B.Ed Restructuring Committee Report*, Toronto, Ontario.

FARBER, B. (1991) *Crisis in Education*, San Francisco, CA, Jossey-Bass.

FEIMAN-NEMSER, S. and PARKER, M. (1992) *Mentoring in Context: A Comparison of Two US Programs for Beginning Teachers*, East Lansing, MI, National Center for Research on Teacher Learning.

FLEXNER, A. (1910) *Medical Education in the United States and Canada*, Washington, DC, Carnegie Foundation for the Advancement of Teaching.

FISKE, E. (1992) *Smart Schools, Smart Kids*, New York, Simon & Schuster.

FORD, D. (1992) 'Principal education and selection in fourteen sample schools', in EASTON, J. (Ed.) *Decision-Making and School Improvement*, Chicago, IL, Chicago Panel on Public School Policy, pp. 16–28.

FULLAN, M. (1988) *What's Worth Fighting for in the Principalship*, Toronto, Ontario, Ontario Public School Teachers' Federation; Andover, MA, The Network; Buckingham, UK, Open University Press; Melbourne, Australia, Australian Council of Educational Administration.

FULLAN, M. (1991) 'The best faculty of education in the country: A fable', submitted to the Strategic Planning Committee. Faculty of Education, University of Toronto.

FULLAN, M. (1992) *Successful School Improvement*, Buckingham, UK, Open University Press.

FULLAN, M. (in press) 'Coordinating school and district development in restructuring', in MURPHY, J. and HALLINGER, P. (Eds) *Restructuring Schools: Learning from Ongoing Efforts*, Newbury Park, CA, Crowin Press.

FULLAN, M., BENNETT, B. and ROLHEISER-BENNETT, C. (1990) 'Linking classroom and school improvement', *Educational Leadership*, 47, 8, pp. 13–19.

FULLAN, M. and HARGREAVES, A. (1991) *What's Worth Fighting for in Your School?*, Toronto, Ontario, Ontario Public School Teachers' Federation; Andover, MA, The Network; Buckingham, UK, Open University Press; Melbourne, Australia, Australian Council of Educational Administration.

FULLAN, M. and MILES, M. (1992) 'Getting reform right: What works and what doesn't', *Phi Delta Kappan* 73, 10, pp. 744–52.

FULLAN, M. with STIEGELBAUER, S. (1991) *The New Meaning of Educational Change*, New York, Teachers College Press.

GARDNER, H. (1991) *The Unschooled Mind*, New York, Basic Books.

GARDNER, J. (1964) *Self-renewal*, New York, Harper & Row.

GLEICK, (1987) *Chaos: Making a New Science*, New York, Penguin Books.

GLICKMAN, C. (in press) *Renewing America's Schools*, San Francisco, CA, Jossey-Bass.

GLICKMAN, C., ALLEN, L. and LUNSFORD, B. (1992) 'Facilitation of internal change: The league of professional schools', paper presented at the annual meeting of the American Educational Research Association, San Francisco.

GOODLAD, J. (1988) 'School-university partnership for educational renewal: Rationale and concepts', in SIROTNIK, K. and GOODLAD, J.I. (Eds) *School-university Partnerships in Action*, New York, Teachers College Press, pp. 3–31.

GOODLAD, J. (1990a) 'Studying the education of educators: From conception to findings', *Phi Delta Kappan*, 71, 9, pp. 698–701.

GOODLAD, J. (1990b) *Teachers for Our Nation's Schools*, San Francisco, CA, Jossey-Bass.

GOODLAD, J. (1991) 'Why we need a complete redesign of teacher education', *Educational Leadership*, 49, 3, pp. 4–10.

GOODLAD, J. (1992a) 'National goals/national testing: The moral dimensions', paper presented at the annual meeting of the American Educational Research Association, San Francisco.

GOODLAD, J. (1992b) 'On taking school reform seriously', *Phi Delta Kappan*, 74, 3, 232–238.

GOODLAD, J., KLEIN, M. and ASSOCIATES (1970) *Behind the Classroom Door*, Worthington, OH, Charles A. Jones.

GOODLAD, J., SODER, R. and SIROTNIK, K.A. (Eds) (1990) *The Moral Dimensions of Teaching*, San Francisco, CA, Jossey-Bass.

GROSS, N., GIACQUINTA, J. and BERNSTEIN, M. (1971) *Implementing Organizational Innovations: A Sociological Analysis of Planned Educational Change*, New York, Basic Books.

GROSSMAN, P. (1992) 'In pursuit of a dual agenda: Creating a middle level professional development school', in DARLING-HAMMOND, L. (Eds) *Professional Development Schools: Schools for Developing a Profession*, New York, Teachers College Press.

HALLINGER, P., MURPHY, J. and HAUSMAN, C. (1991) 'Conceptualizing school restructuring: Principals' and teachers' perceptions', paper presented at the annual meeting of the American Educational Research Association, Chicago.

HAMPDEN-TURNER, C. (1992) 'Charting the dilemmas of Hanover Insurance', *Planning Review*, January–February, pp. 22–8.

HARGREAVES, A. and TUCKER, E. (1991) 'Teaching and Guilt: Exploring the feelings of teachers', unpublished paper, Toronto, Ontario, Ontario Institute for Studies in Education.

HART, A. (1992) 'Work feature values of tomorrow's teachers: Work redesign as an incentive and school improvement policy', paper presented at the annual meeting of the American Educational Research Association, San Francisco.

HART, A.W. and MURPHY, M.J. (1990) 'New teachers react to redesigned teacher work', *American Journal of Education*, 98, pp. 224–50.

HARVEY, J. (1989) *The Abilene Paradox*, San Diego, CA, University Associates.

HILL, P. and BONAN, J. (1991) *Decentralization and Accountability in Public Education*, Santa Monica, CA, Rand.

HODGKINSON, H. (1991) 'Reform versus reality', *Phi Delta Kappan*, 72, 1, pp. 9–16.

HOLMES GROUP (1986) *Tomorrow's Teachers*, East Lansing, MI.

HOLMES GROUP (1990) *Tomorrow's Schools*, East Lansing, MI.

HOLMES GROUP (in press) *Tomorrow's Colleges of Education*, East Lansing, MI.

HOWEY, K.R. (1992) *The Network of Fifteen*, Columbus, OH, Ohio State University, unpublished proposal.

HOWEY, K.R. and ZIMPHER, N.L. (1989) *Profiles of Preservice Teacher Education, Inquiry into the Nature of Programs*, Albany, NY, State University of New York Press.

HUBERMAN, M. (1992) 'Teacher development and instructional mastery', in HARGREAVES, A. and FULLAN, M. (Eds) *Understanding Teacher Development*, New York: Teachers College Press, pp. 122–42.

JANIS, I. (1972) *Victims of Groupthink*, Boston, MA, Houghton, Mifflin.

JETT-SIMPSON, M., PUGACH, M. and WHIP, J. (1992) 'Portrait of an urban professional development school', paper presented at the annual meeting of the American Educational Research Association, San Francisco.

JEUINE, R. and ZINGLE, H. (1992) *Striving for Health: Living with Broken Dreams*, Edmonton, Alberta: Alberta School Employee Benefit Plan.

KANTER, R.M., STEIN, B. and JICK, T. (1992) *The Challenge of Organizational Change*, New York, The Free Press.

KAPLAN, R. (1991) *Beyond Ambition*, San Francisco, CA, Jossey-Bass.

KRAMER, R. (1992) *Ed School Follies*, New York, Foss Press.

LACEY, V. (1991) 'Restructuring preservice teacher education', unpublished paper, Toronto, North York Board of Education.

LAING, P. (1992) 'Administrative workshop', unpublished paper, Oshawa, Ontario, Durham Board of Education.

LAND, G. and JARMAN, B. (1992) *Break-point and Beyond*, New York, Harper Business.

LEITHWOOD, K. (1992) 'The move toward transformational leadership', *Educational Leadership*, 49, 5, pp. 8–12.

LESSING, D. (1986) *Prisons We Choose to Live Inside*, Toronto, CBC Enterprises.

LEVIN, H. (1988) 'Accelerating elementary education for disadvantaged students', in Chief State School Officers (Eds) *School Success for Students at Risk*, Orlando, FL, Harcourt, Brace, Jovanovich, pp. 209–25.

LICHTENSTEIN, G., RUBIN, T. and GRANT, G. (1992) 'Teacher portfolios and professional development', paper presented at the annual meeting of the American Educational Research Association, San Francisco.

LICHTENSTEIN, G., McLAUGLIN, M. and KNUDSEN, J. (1992) 'Teacher empowerment and professional knowledge', in LIEBERMAN, A. (Ed.) *The Changing Contexts of Teaching*, Chicago, University of Chicago Press, pp. 37–58.

LIEBERMAN, A., DARLING-HAMMOND, L. and ZUCKERMAN, D. (1991) *Early Lessons in Restructuring Schools*, New York, NY, National Center for Restructuring Education, Schools, and Teaching.

LIEBERMAN, A. and McLAUGLIN, M. (1992) 'Networks for educational change: Powerful and problematic', *Kappan* 73, 9, pp. 673–7.

LISTON, D. and ZEICHNER, K. (1991) *Teacher Education and the Social Conditions of Schooling*, New York, Routledge, Chapman and Hall.

LORTIE, D. (1975) *School Teacher: A Sociological Study*, Chicago IL, University of Chicago Press.

LOUIS, K. and MILES, M.B. (1990) *Improving the Urban High School: What Works and Why*, New York, Teachers College Press.

McCARTHY, J. (1992) 'The effect of the accelerated schools process on individual teachers' decision-making and instructional strategies', paper presented at the annual meeting of the American Educational Research Association, San Francisco.

McDONALD, J. (1992) *Teaching: Making Sense of an Uncertain Craft*, New York, Teachers College Press.

McDONALD, J. and ELIAS, P. (1980) *The Problems of Beginning Teachers: A Crisis in Training* (Vol. 1), Princeton, NJ, Educational Testing Service.

McLAUGHLIN, M. (1990) 'The Rand Change Agent Study revisited', *Educational Researcher*, 5, pp. 11–16.

McLAUGHLIN, M. (1992) *Employability Skills Profile: What are Employers Looking For?* The Conference Board of Canada, Ottawa, Canada.

McMAHON, A. and WALLACE, M. (1992) 'Planning for development in multiracial primary schools', paper presented at the annual meeting of the American Educational Research Association, San Francisco.

MANTHEI, J. (1992) 'The mentor teacher as leader: The motives, characteristics and needs of seventy-three experienced teachers who see a new leadership role', paper presented at the Annual Meeting of the American Educational Research Association, San Francisco.

MARRIS, P. (1975) *Loss and Change*, New York, Anchor Press/Doubleday.

MECKLENBERGER, J. (1992) The braking of the 'break-the-mold' express, *Phi Delta Kappan*, 74, 4, pp. 280–289.

METRO TORONTO LEARNING PARTNERSHIP (1992) Toronto, Canada.

MURPHY, J. (1991) *Restructuring Schools*, New York, NY, Teachers College Press.

NAISBITT, J. and ABERDENE, P. (1990) *Megatrends 2000*, New York, William Morrow.

NATIONAL ALLIANCE OF BUSINESS (1989) *A Blueprint for Business on Restructuring Education*, Washington, DC, NAB.

NATIONAL BOARD FOR PROFESSIONAL TEACHING STANDARDS (1992) *Toward High and Rigorous Standards for the Profession*, Detroit, MI, NBPTS.

NATIONAL COMMISSION ON EXCELLENCE IN EDUCATION (1983) *A Nation at Risk*, Washington, DC, NCEE.

THE NETWORK (1991) *Study of Teacher Professionalism and Professionalism of Other School Personnel: From Progress to Systemic Approaches*, Andover, MA, The Network.

NEW BRUNSWICK DEPARTMENT OF EDUCATION (1992) *Excellence in Education: The Challenge*, St. John, New Brunswick, Department of Education.

NIAS, J., SOUTHWORTH, G. and CAMPBELL, P. (1992) *Whole School Curriculum Development in the Primary School*, Lewes, Falmer Press.

NIAS, J., SOUTHWORTH, G. and YEOMANS, R. (1989) *Staff Relationships in the Primary School*, London, Cassell.

OFFORD, D., BOYLE, M. and RACINE, Y. (1991) 'Children at risk: Schools reaching out', *Education Today*, March/April, pp. 17–18.

ONTARIO TEACHERS' FEDERATION (OTF) (1992a) *Beyond the Glitterspeak*, The 1992 Submission to the Cabinet, Toronto, Ontario, Ontario Teachers Federation.

ONTARIO TEACHERS' FEDERATION (OTF) (1992b) *Creating a Culture for Change*, Toronto, Ontario, Ontario Teachers' Federation.

PASCALE, P. (1990) *Managing on the Edge*, New York, Touchstone.

PETERS, T. (1992) *Liberation Management*, New York, A. Knopf.

PRESTINE, N. (1992) 'Benchmarks of change: Assessing essential school restructuring efforts', paper presented at the annual meeting of the American Educational Research Association, San Francisco.

PRESTINE, N. (in press) 'Feeling the ripples, riding the waves: Making an essential school', in MURPHY, J. and HALLINGER, P. (Eds) *Restructuring Schools: Learning from Ongoing Efforts*, Newbury Park, CA, Corwin Press.

PUGACH, M. and PASCH, S. (1992) 'The challenge of creating urban professional development schools', paper presented at the annual meeting of the American Educational Research Association, San Francisco.

ROSENHOLTZ, S. (1989) *Teachers' Workplace: The Social Organization of Schools*, New York, Longman.

ROTHSCHILD, J. (1990) 'Feminist values and the democratic management of work organizations', paper presented at the 12th World Congress of Sociology, Madrid.

RUDDUCK, J. (1992) 'Universities in partnership with schools and school systems: Les liaisons dangereuses?', in FULLAN, M. and HARGREAVES, A. (Eds) *Teacher Development and Educational Change*, Lewes, Falmer Press, pp. 194–212.

SARASON, S. (1971) *The Culture of the School and the Problem of Change*, Boston, MA, Allyn & Bacon.

SARASON, S. (1990) *The Predictable Failure of Educational Reform*, San Francisco, CA, Jossey-Bass.

SARASON, S. (in press) *The Case for a Change; The Preparation of Educators*, San Francisco, CA, Jossey-Bass.

SAUL, J.R. (1992) *Voltaire's Bastards: The Dictatorship of Reason in the West*, New York, The Free Press.

SCHLECHTY, P. (1990) *Reform in Teacher Education*, Washington DC, American Association of Colleges of Education.

SCHRAGE, M. (1990) *Shared Minds*, New York, Random House.

SENGE, P. (1990) *The Fifth Discipline*, New York, Doubleday.

SERGIOVANNI, T. (1992) *Moral Leadership*, San Francisco, CA, Jossey-Bass.

SHAKESHAFT, C. (1987) *Women in Educational Administration*, Beverly Hills, CA, Sage.

SHANKER, A. (1990) 'Staff development and the restructured school', in JOYCE, B. (Ed.) *Changing School Culture Through Staff Development*, Alexandria, VA, Association for Supervision and Curriculum Development, pp. 91–103.

SHEPARD, L. (1991) 'Will national tests improve student learning?', *Phi Delta Kappan*, 72, 3, pp. 232–8.

SIROTNIK, K. (1990) 'Society, schooling, teaching, and preparing to teach', in GOODLAD, J., SODER, R. and SIROTNIK, K. (Eds) *The Moral Dimensions of Teaching*, San Francisco, CA, Jossey-Bass, pp. 296–327.

SIZER, T. (1991) 'No pain, no gain', *Educational Leadership*, 48, 8, pp. 32–4.

SIZER, T. (1992) *Horace's School: Redesigning the American High School*, Boston, MA, Houghton Mifflin.

SMITH, K. (1984) 'Rabbits, lynxes, and organizational transitions', in KIMBERLEY, J. and QUINN, R. (Eds) *Managing Organizational Transitions*, Homewood, IL, Irwin.

SMYLIE, M. and BROWNLEE-CONYERS, J. (1992) 'Teacher leaders and their principals', *Education Administration Quarterly*, 28, 2, pp. 150–84.

STACEY, R. (1992) *Managing the Unknowable*, San Francisco, CA, Jossey-Bass.

STEVENSON, H. and STIGLER, J. (1992) *The Learning Gap*, New York, Summit Books.

STIEGELBAUER, S. (1992) 'Why we want to be teachers', paper presented at the annual meeting of the American Educational Research Association, San Francisco.

STODDART, T., WINITZKY, N. and O'KEEFE, P. (1992) 'Developing the professional development school', paper presented at the annual meeting of the American Educational Research Association, San Francisco.

STORR, A. (1988) *Solitude*, London, Flamingo Press.

TAYLOR, D. and TEDDLIE, C. (1992) 'Restructuring and the classroom: A view from a reform district', paper presented at the annual meeting of the American Educational Research Association, San Francisco.

TOCH, T. (1991) *In the Name of Excellence*, New York, Oxford University Press.

TUCHMAN, B. (1984) *The March of Folly*, New York, A. Knopf.

VERSPOOR, A. (1989) *Pathways to Change*, Washington DC, World Bank.

WALLACE, M. (1991) 'Contradictory interests in policy implementation: The case of LEA development plans for schools', *Journal of Educational Policy*, 6, 4, pp. 385–400.

WASLEY, P. (1991) *Teachers who Lead*, New York, Teachers College Press.

WATSON, N. and FULLAN, M. (1992) 'Beyond school district-university partnerships', in FULLAN, M. and HARGREAVES, A. (Eds) *Teacher Development and Educational Change*, Lewes, Falmer Press, pp. 213–42.

WATTS, G. and CASTLE, S. (1992) 'Electronic networking and the construction of professional knowledge', *Kappan*, 75, 9, pp. 684–9.

WEHLAGE, G., SMITH, G. and LIPMAN, P. (1992) 'Restructuring urban high schools: The New Futures Experience', *American Educational Research Journal*, 29, 1, pp. 51–93.

WEINER, L. (1992) 'Preparing teachers for a new educational paradigm: Lessons from the 1960s', paper presented at the annual meeting of the American Educational Research Association, San Francisco.

WEISS, C. (1992) 'Shared decision making about what? A comparison of schools with and without teacher participation', paper presented at the annual meeting of the American Educational Research Association, San Francisco.

WHEATLEY, M. (1992) *Leadership and the New Science*, San Francisco, CA, Berrett-Koehler Publishers.

WINITZKY, N., STODDART, T. and O'KEEFE, P. (1992) 'Great expectations: Emergent professional development schools', *Journal of Teacher Education*, 43, 1, pp. 3–18.

WISE, A. (1988) 'The two conflicting trends in school reform: Legislative learning revisited', *Phi Delta Kappan*, 69, 5, pp. 328–33.

YI, Y. and MA, L. (1992) 'Teacher education conducted by teacher community: A case of mentoring in China', paper presented at the annual meeting of the American Educational Research Association, San Francisco.

Index